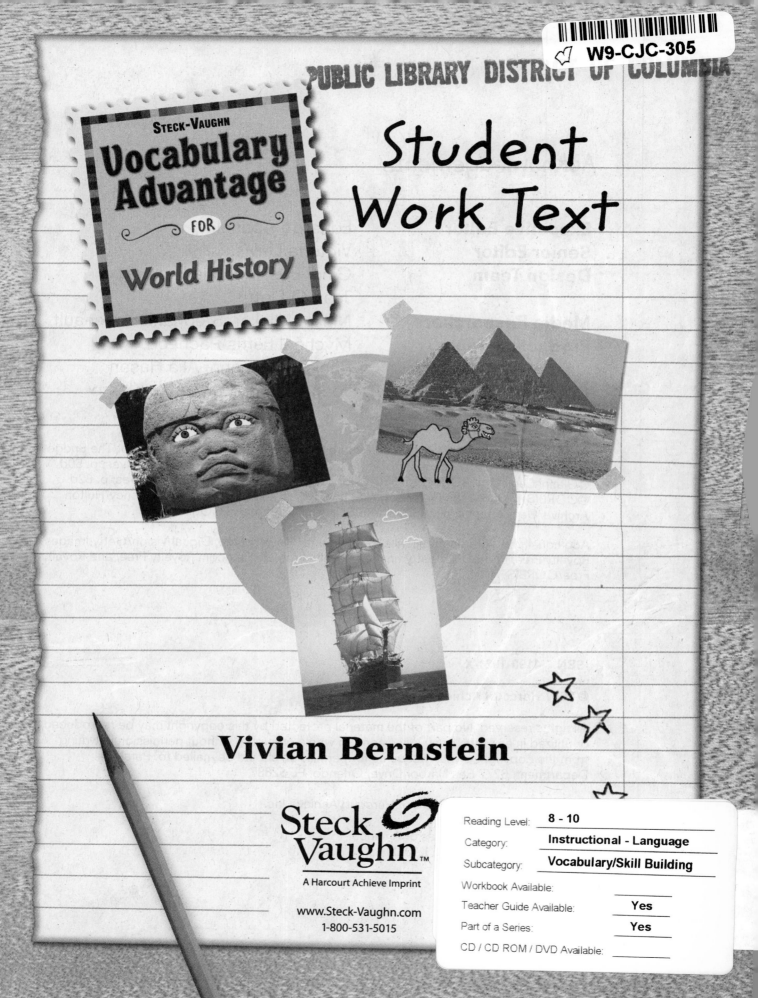

STECK-VAUGHN
Vocabulary Advantage
FOR
World History

Student Work Text

Vivian Bernstein

Steck Vaughn™
A Harcourt Achieve Imprint

www.Steck-Vaughn.com
1-800-531-5015

Reading Level:	8 - 10
Category:	Instructional - Language
Subcategory:	Vocabulary/Skill Building
Workbook Available:	
Teacher Guide Available:	Yes
Part of a Series:	Yes
CD / CD ROM / DVD Available:	

Acknowledgements

Executive Editor	Eduardo Aparicio
Senior Editor	Victoria Davis
Design Team	Cindi Ellis, Cynthia Hannon, Jean O'Dette
Media Researchers	Nicole Mlakar, Stephanie Arsenault
Production Team	Mychael Ferris-Pacheco, Paula Schumann, Alia Hasan
Creative Team	Joan Cunningham, Alan Klemp

Photo Credits

Page 20d ©North Wind/North Wind Picture Archives; p. 26d ©Spanish School/The Bridgeman Art Library/Getty Images; p. 44d ©North Wind/North Wind Picture Archives; p. 50d ©Gianni Dagli Orti/CORBIS; p. 56d ©North Wind/North Wind Picture Archives; p. 62d ©CORBIS; p. 68d ©The Granger Collection, NY; p. 74d ©Topical Press Agency/Hulton Archive/Getty Images; p. 80d ©CORBIS; p. 86d ©Bettmann/CORBIS.

Additional photography by Artville/Getty Images Royalty Free, Digital Vision/Getty Images Royalty Free, PhotoDisc/Getty Images Royalty Free, Photos.com Royalty Free, and Royalty-Free/CORBIS.

ISBN 1-4190-1921-X

Dear Student,

Welcome to _Vocabulary Advantage for World History_!

In this Student Work Text, you will

- learn new history words that will help you better understand what you read in your history textbook,

- learn useful words that will help you in the classroom and on tests, and

- learn skills that will help you figure out the meaning of other new words.

You will write and talk about the new words you've learned. You should also feel free to draw, circle, underline, and make notes on the pages of this Work Text to help you remember what the new words mean. You can do more writing and drawing in your World History Vocabulary Journal.

All of the tools in this book will help you build your own understanding of important history and classroom vocabulary. Building your understanding of these words will give you an advantage in your history class and on history tests!

Have fun!

Table of Contents

Lesson 1 Beginnings of Civilization

Read the passage below. Think about the meanings of the new words printed in **bold**. Underline any definitions that might help you figure out what these words mean. The first one has been done for you.

Vocabulary Strategy

Writers will often include definitions of new or difficult words near those words in a text. Look for definitions in the text to help you understand new words.

Early People

The first people lived thousands of years ago. They lived during **prehistoric** times, or the <u>period before people learned how to write their languages</u>. We have learned a lot about the way early people lived from the work of **archaeologists**. Archaeologists are scientists who study the past by finding **artifacts**, or objects that were made by people long ago. The **significance**, or importance, of artifacts is that they tell us how people lived long ago.

The first people lived in Africa. They lived in a world that had no stores and no electricity. These early people learned to hunt animals. They made clothing from animal skins.

They also found plants, nuts, and berries that they ate to survive.

The first people were **nomads**, people who move from place to place. When they could no longer find food in one place, they moved to another. Wherever they lived, they always began a new search for food.

New World History Words

archaeology

noun   the study of the buildings, tools, and way of life of people of the past

artifact

noun   a tool or object that is made by and used by a person

nomad

noun   a person who moves from place to place to find food

prehistoric

noun   people and things that existed before history was written down

Now read this passage and practice the vocabulary strategy again. Underline any definitions in the passage that help you figure out what the new words in **bold** mean.

The Beginning of Village Life

It was difficult for early people to live as nomads. Life became easier when people learned to use fire. Fire helped them cook food and stay warm.

Life became easier when early people learned to **cultivate**, or grow, fruits and vegetables. They learned to **differentiate**, or tell the difference, between plants that were safe and those that contained poison. They also learned to **domesticate**, or tame, wild animals. They tamed pigs, dogs, horses, and goats. Some animals were used to help with farm work. Others were used for food.

As early people learned to farm, **migration**, or movement, took place from Africa to other places. People migrated to Asia, the Middle East, and to other places. The early farmers learned to live and work together in villages. They developed **cultures**. A culture is the shared traditions and beliefs of a group of people. As time passed, some of these early cultures developed into civilizations. You will read more about early civilizations in Lesson 2.

How do you like being **domesticated**?

The work's hard, but I like the **culture**.

More New World History Words

cultivate
  verb   to prepare land to grow crops, or to develop something to make it better

culture
  noun   the shared traditions and beliefs of a group of people

domesticate
  verb   to tame animals and grow plants for human use

migration
  noun   movement from one region or country to another

Other Useful Words

differentiate
  verb   to show the difference between things

significance
  noun   importance

Apply the Strategy

Look at a chapter in your textbook that your teacher identifies. Use definitions in the text to help you figure out the meaning of any new words you find.

Find the Word

Write a word from the box next to each clue. Then write the word formed by the boxed letters to finish the sentence below.

domesticate	culture	migration	nomad
artifact	archaeology	prehistoric	

1 movement from one region or country to another ___ ___ ___ □ ___ ___ ___ ___ ___

2 a group's shared traditions and beliefs ___ ___ ___ ___ ___ ___ □

3 to tame animals ___ ___ □ ___ ___ ___ ___ ___ ___ ___

4 the study of past people □ ___ ___ ___ ___ ___ ___ ___ ___ ___

5 tool or object made and used by a person ___ ___ ___ ___ □ ___ ___ ___

6 someone who moves from place to place □ ___ ___ ___ ___

7 before history was written ___ ___ ___ ___ ___ □ ___ ___ ___ ___ ___

Archaeologists study people of the past by looking at ___ ___ ___ ___ ___ ___ ___ ___.

Word Challenge: Word Associations

Take turns with a partner reading the groups of words below. Write the word from the lesson that goes best with each group.

1 _____artifact_____ a stone axe, clay bowls, arrowheads

2 _____ importance, value, meaning

3 _____ tame, control, train

4 _____ to tell apart, separate, difference

Word Challenge: Quick Pick

Read each question with a partner or by yourself. Think of a response and write it on the line. Explain your answer.

1 Which is an **artifact**: a plant or a stone axe? _A stone axe is an artifact_

because a person made it.

2 Is a person who moves a lot a **nomad** or are they **prehistoric**? _____

_____

3 If you wanted to train a dog, would you **domesticate** or **cultivate** it? _____

_____

4 In **archaeology**, would you study an ancient pot or a modern map? _____

_____

Analogies

Use a word from the box to finish each sentence. Write the word on the line. Discuss your answers with a partner.

domesticate	nomad	archaeology	prehistoric

1 Artifacts are to _____ as rocks are to geology.

2 Tame is to _____ as act is to perform.

3 Govern is to politician as travel is to _____.

4 Ancient is to _____ as fit is to athletic.

Word Study: The Suffix *-ation*

When the suffix *-ation* is added to a verb such as *migrate*, it does two things:

- First, it changes the verb to a noun: *migration*.
- Second, it changes the word's meaning. The word now means "movement from one region or country to another."

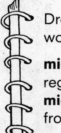

Drop the *-e* from the end of a word before adding *-ation*.

migrate (v.) to move from one region or country to another
migration (n.) movement from one region or country to another

A. Add *-ation* to the following root words to make a new word and write a definition for each. Use a dictionary to check your spelling and your definitions.

		+ *-ation*	Definition
1	cultivate		
2	domesticate		
3	examine		

B. Write a new *-ation* word from above in each blank.

1 The _____ of animals allows us to have pets.

2 The process of preparing land to grow crops is called _____.

6

The Language of Testing

How would you answer a question like this on a test?

Identify a fact that tells you a group of people were prehistoric.

    A. They weren't very strong.
    B. They didn't use tools.
    C. They lived before people could write.
    D. They couldn't walk very far.

Tip

When you *identify*, you point out or name something. In a test question, the word *identify* means that you need to choose or pick the correct answer.

Test Strategy: Make sure you understand the question. Read it carefully. If you see a question that uses the word *identify*, rewrite it using the words *choose* or *pick*.

1 How could you say the question above in a different way?

_____

_____

Try the strategy again by asking these questions in a different way.

2 Identify the correct definition for the word *nomads*.

    A. People who move from place to place.
    B. People who lived before history was written down.
    C. People who study the past.
    D. People who make objects or tools.

3 Identify something that has to do with *migration*.

    A. creating a new set of beliefs
    B. growing new crops
    C. moving to a new country
    D. buying a new home

_____ _____

_____ _____

_____ _____

In Your Vocabulary Journal

Find each of these words in your World History Vocabulary Journal. Working by yourself or with a partner, use the definitions from pages 2 and 3 of your Work Text to complete the rest of the entry for each word.

archaeology	artifact	cultivate	culture	differentiate
domesticate	migration	nomad	prehistoric	significance

Read the passage below. Decide if each new word in **bold** is a noun or verb. In the space above each new word, write *noun* or *verb*. Four of the new words in the passage are nouns. The first one has been done for you. Use this information with other clues in the text to figure out what each new word means.

Vocabulary Strategy

Identify if a new word is used as a noun, verb, adjective, or adverb to help you use other clues in the text to figure out the meaning of the new words.

Early People

About 7,000 years ago, the people of Egypt developed their own culture along the Nile River. Egypt is a hot dry country, but water from the Nile made it possible to farm the land.

noun
Egypt's government was an **autocracy**. The **pharaoh**, or king, had total power to make laws. Egypt's government also had a large **bureaucracy**. In a bureaucracy, people do many different kinds of jobs for the government.

The people of Egypt practiced **polytheism**, which means that they believed in many gods. Their most important god was the sun god. They also believed the pharaoh was a god.

The Egyptians built huge pyramids as tombs for the pharaohs. These pyramids were in the shape of triangles. Thousands of slaves built each pyramid. The pyramids were built so well that they have lasted for thousands of years. The art and objects inside these pyramids **verify**, or prove, these facts about life along the Nile long ago.

New World History Words

autocracy
> *noun*   a government controlled by one person who has total power

bureaucracy
> *noun*   all of the rules followed by a government department, or a system in which many people in many jobs help run the government

pharaoh
> *noun*   a king in ancient Egypt

polytheism
> *noun*   belief in more than one god

Now read the passage below and practice the vocabulary strategy again. Write *noun*, *verb*, or *adjective* above each new word.

Other Ancient Civilizations

Civilizations developed in many parts of the world. These **ancient**, or old, civilizations had art, music, religion, cities, and governments. Most ancient people prayed to many gods. The Jews however, were one group of people that believed in only one god. A belief in one god is called **monotheism**. The Jews also believed that their god wanted people to be honest and kind. Jews lived in the land that is now called Israel.

The ancient Persians conquered other countries and built a large **empire**. An empire is made up of a number of countries that have one ruler. Every part of the huge Persian empire had to obey the same laws.

Another great civilization developed in China. China was ruled by **dynasties**. A dynasty is a family of rulers. Sometimes the same dynasty ruled China for hundreds of years. The Chinese created beautiful art and cloth. They also spread important ideas. However, another **relevant**, or important, fact about Chinese culture is their respect for family life. Children learn to respect their parents and grandparents at an early age. Respect for parents and grandparents continues to be important in China today.

The family's an **autocracy**!

No, we're more of a **bureaucracy**. We all have jobs to do, and yours is to take out the trash.

More New World History Words

ancient
adjective   belonging to the distant past

dynasty
noun   a ruling family

empire
noun   a number of countries that are all under the control of one ruling country

monotheism
noun   a belief in one god

Other Useful Words

relevant
adjective   relating to something

verify
verb   using evidence to check if something is true

Apply the Strategy

Look at a chapter in your textbook that your teacher identifies. Identify parts of speech to help you figure out the meaning of any new words you find.

Finish the Sentence

Use a word from the box to finish each sentence. Write the correct word on the line. Discuss your choices with a partner.

ancient	autocracy	bureaucracy	dynasties
empire	monotheism	pharaohs	polytheism

1. Ancient China was ruled by _____, or families of rulers.

2. The pyramids of ancient Egypt were built for the _____.

3. The Middle East was home to many _____ civilizations that were started thousands of years ago.

4. The country was an _____, because it was run by an all-powerful ruler.

5. Rome was a great _____ because it controlled many lands.

6. Christians, Muslims, and Jews follow _____, the belief in one god.

7. A _____ is a government with many different people making many decisions.

8. Many early people practiced _____, or the belief in many gods.

Word Challenge: True or False

Take turns with a partner reading the sentences below out loud. Write **T** next to each sentence that is true. Write **F** next to each sentence that is false. Rewrite each false sentence. The first one has been done for you.

1. __F__ An **ancient** piece of furniture could have been made in the past ten years.

   An ancient piece of furniture was made a thousand years ago.

2. _____ Early Greeks practiced **polytheism** because they believed in one god.

   _____

3. _____ A **dynasty** is a period of time when a country is ruled by leaders from the same family.

   _____

4. _____ You can use evidence to **verify** if something is true.

   _____

Word Challenge: What's Your Answer?

Take turns with a partner reading each question out loud and writing an answer on the line. Answer the questions in complete sentences. The first one has been done for you.

1. Where would a **pharaoh** have lived? _A pharaoh would have lived_

   in Egypt.

2. What kind of information is **relevant** to your life? _____

   _____

3. Why might politicians and citizens want less **bureaucracy**? _____

   _____

4. What is the most important belief in **monotheism**? _____

   _____

11

Word Connections

Write at the top of the circle the words from the box that connect to the word or idea in the center. Write the words that do not connect in the blue area at the bottom. Discuss your choices with a partner.

relevant	autocracy	bureaucracy
pharaoh	monotheism	verify

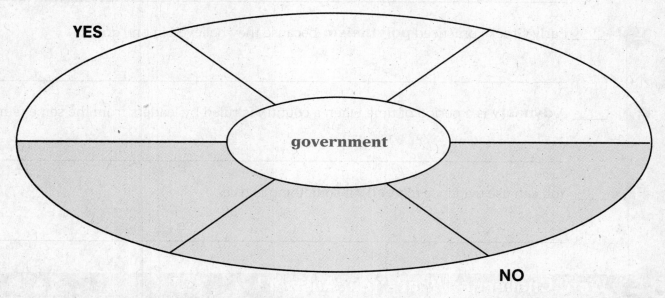

YES

government

NO

Word Study: The Prefixes *mono-* and *poly-*

When the prefixes *mono-* and *poly-* are added to a word, such as *tone*, they change the meaning of the word. *Mono-* means *one* or *single*. *Poly-* means *many*.

tone (n.) the pitch or sound of a voice
monotone (n.) made up of one tone
polytone (n.) made up of many tones

Circle each root word. Underline the prefixes *mono-* and *poly-*. Write a sentence for each word. Use a dictionary if you need help.

1 monosyllable _____

2 polysyllable _____

3 monotheism _____

4 polytheism _____

The Language of Testing

How would you answer a question like this on a test?

Which of the following describes the word *bureaucracy*?

A. the rules of a government department
B. a government ruled by one person
C. leadership by the people
D. a government made up of family members

 Tip

The phrase *which of the following* means that you need to choose one of the answers listed (A, B, C, or D) to answer the question.

Test Strategy: If the question has the phrase *which of the following* in it, ask the question in a different way. Start your restated question with *what, who,* or *where.*

1 How could you say the question above in a different way?

_____

_____

Try the strategy again by asking these questions in a different way.

2 Which of the following in not a true statement about a pharaoh?

A. Pharaohs were rulers.
B. Pharaohs were Egyptian.
C. Pharaohs ruled long ago.
D. Pharaohs were always female.

_____

_____

3 Which of the following words is not related to leading a country?

A. autocracy
B. polytheism
C. dynasty
D. bureaucracy

_____

_____

In Your Vocabulary Journal

Find each of these words in your World History Vocabulary Journal. Working by yourself or with a partner, use the definitions from pages 8 and 9 of your Work Text to complete the rest of the entry for each word.

ancient	autocracy	bureaucracy	dynasty	empire
monotheism	pharaoh	polytheism	relevant	verify

Lesson 3
Greek and Roman Civilizations

Read the passage below. Think about the meaning of the words printed in **bold**. Underline any words that end with -*cy*. Remember that -*cy* names a type of government. Write what you think each word means near it. The first one has been done for you.

Ancient Greece

Vocabulary Strategy

Use familiar prefixes and suffixes to help you understand the meanings of new words.

government of wealthy people

Athens was the most important city of ancient Greece. At one time, Athens was an **aristocracy**, a government that is controlled by rich people, or aristocrats. Later, Athens became the world's first **democracy**, a government that is ruled by all people. Rich people and poor people had the same right to vote and make laws in Athens.

Like other people long ago, the Greeks believed in many gods. They told interesting stories called myths about their gods. These ancient stories have been **paraphrased**, or rewritten, in simple language. Children today enjoy reading these very old stories.

The Greeks also studied **philosophy**. Philosophy is the study of ideas about knowledge and life. One part of Greek philosophy said it was important to develop both a strong mind and a strong body.

The Greeks also spoke about their ideas in public. Many Greeks used **rhetoric** to convince others that they had the right ideas about knowledge and life.

✔ New World History Words

aristocracy
 noun a class of people who have high position in society

democracy
 noun a system of government in which people choose their own laws and leaders

philosophy
 noun the study of ideas

rhetoric
 noun the use of language to convince people about something

Now read this passage and underline any words that begin with *pre-* or *de-*. Write what you think each of the circled words means next to it. Remember that *pre-* means *before*, and *de-* means *down*.

Ancient Rome

The city of Rome began in Italy about 2500 years ago. The Romans built the largest empire in the ancient world. They believed their empire would last forever. The Romans could not **predict** that after 800 years, their empire would break apart.

The Romans did not want to be ruled by a king or queen, so they started a government that was a **republic**. In a republic, people vote for their leaders. But rich Romans had more power in the government than poor people. Sometimes the leader of the government was a **dictator**. A dictator has full power to lead the army and make laws.

While the Roman Empire grew larger, the Christian religion began. The new religion was based on the teachings of Jesus. Jesus was a Jew who taught people to believe in one God. He also stressed the importance of **ethics**, beliefs and rules about what is right and wrong.

The huge Roman Empire slowly **declined**, or grew weaker. About 1500 years ago, the Roman empire broke apart.

More New World History Words

decline

verb to become less in amount or importance

noun a process by which something becomes less in amount or importance

dictator

noun a leader who has total control in a country

ethics

noun beliefs and rules about what is right and wrong

republic

noun a country where people have the power

Our **republic** is shrinking.

I **predict** we are in a terrible **decline**.

Other Useful Words

paraphrase

verb to reword something spoken or written

predict

verb to say what will happen in the future

Apply the Strategy

Look at a chapter in your textbook that your teacher identifies. Use familiar prefixes and suffixes to help you figure out the meaning of any new words you find.

Matching

Finish the sentences in Group A with words from Group B. Discuss your answers with a partner.

Group A

1. Julius Caesar is called a _____ because he had total control of Rome.

2. The Greeks invented _____ when they began to choose their leaders.

3. Politicians use _____ in their speeches to convince people to vote for them.

4. Can you _____ what the weather will be like tomorrow?

5. The Greek thinker Socrates shared his _____ about life in a dialogue with Plato.

Group B

A. democracy

B. dictator

C. predict

D. philosophy

E. rhetoric

Group A

6. People consider _____ when they make important decisions about life.

7. When people had a role in government, Rome was called a _____.

8. Roman society was broken up into classes with the _____ at the top and slaves at the bottom.

9. Possible reasons for the _____ of the Roman empire include money and military problems.

10. Persis _____ the long book for me so I would not have to read the whole thing.

Group B

F. aristocracy

G. decline

H. paraphrased

I. ethics

J. republic

Word Challenge: What's Your Answer?

Take turns with a partner reading each question out loud and writing an answer on the line. Answer the questions with complete sentences. The first one has been done for you.

1 When might you use **rhetoric**? _I use rhetoric when I want to convince someone._

2 What rights might you lose if you lived in a country ruled by a **dictator**? _____

_____

3 What is one characteristic of a **democracy**? _____

_____

4 Who has the power in a **republic**? _____

_____

Word Challenge: Which Word?

With a partner, take turns saying the words listed below. Together, think of a statement for each one that gives a clue about its meaning. Write your statement next to the word. The first one has been done for you.

1 aristocracy _"I am a member of a wealthy and powerful class."_

2 ethics _____

3 paraphrase _____

4 philosophy _____

Synonyms and Antonyms

Write either a synonym or antonym for the vocabulary words below. In some cases, you might be able to write both. Discuss your answers with a partner.

	Synonym	Antonym
1 predict		
2 decline		
3 democracy		
4 dictator		

Word Study: The Suffixes -er and -or

When a suffix -er or -or is added to a root verb such as *dictate,* it does two things:

- First, it changes the part of speech from a verb to a noun: *dictator.*
- Second, it changes the meaning of the word. The new word names a person or thing that does a job.

dictate (v.) to order or command
dictator (n.) a person who rules a country with total control

Add -er or -or to the words below. Write the new word. Give the meaning of the new word you made. Use a dictionary to check your spelling and definitions.

	+ -er or -or	Definition
1 predict		
2 philosophy		
3 empire		
4 cultivate		

The Language of Testing

How would you answer a question like this on a test?

Each of the following statements is true

(**except**)

    A. Rhetoric is used in persuasive speeches.
    B. A dictator has total control.
    C. A philosophy is a rule about what is right and wrong.
    D. Aristocrats hold a high position in society.

 Tip

The word *except* means you should look for something that means the opposite of the word or phrase before *except*. The opposite of true is false. So in this question, you should look for the answer that is false.

Test Strategy: Make sure you understand the question. Read it carefully. Then, if it has the word *except* in it, ask the question in a different way. Remember that you are looking for the statement that is false.

1 How could you say the question above in a different way?

_____

_____

Try the strategy again by asking these questions in a different way.

2 Each of these words is related to government except

    A. dictator
    B. democracy
    C. republic
    D. philosophy

3 All of these words describe aristocrats except

    A. blue-collar
    B. noble
    C. powerful
    D. upper class

_____

_____

_____

_____

_____

_____

In Your Vocabulary Journal

Find each of these words in your World History Vocabulary Journal. Working by yourself or with a partner, use the definitions from pages 14 and 15 of your Work Text to complete the rest of the entry for each word.

aristocracy	**decline**	**democracy**	**dictator**	**ethics**
paraphrase	**philosophy**	**predict**	**republic**	**rhetoric**

Lesson 4 Medieval Life in Europe

Read the passage below. Think about the meanings of the new words printed in **bold**. Underline each definition and draw a line from it to the word it defines. The first one has been done for you.

Life in the Middle Ages

Vocabulary Strategy

Look for definitions in the text to help you figure out the meaning of new words you find.

The years in Europe from 500 to 1500 were called the Middle Ages. They were also called **medieval** times. During this time, kings became less powerful.

A system called **feudalism** began during this period. Under this system, kings gave land to nobles. In return, nobles promised that their soldiers would fight for the king. The nobles also promised to protect the people who worked on their land. The large house and the land that belonged to the noble was called the **manor**. A manor had a church, farms, and a village.

During the Middle Ages, the Catholic Church became very powerful. Most people in Europe belonged to the church. But some people did not agree with Catholic teachings and tried to **refute** them. Catholic leaders called people who did not follow its teachings **heretics**. Many heretics were punished during the Middle Ages.

New World History Words

feudalism

noun a system in which people were given land to work on and were protected by people with more power

heretic

noun someone whose beliefs and actions go against accepted beliefs

manor

noun a large country house on a large area of land with several smaller buildings around it

medieval

adjective describing something belonging to the period of time in Europe between AD 476 and AD 1500

Now read the passage below and practice the strategy again. Underline *four* definitions in the text that can help you figure out what the words in bold print mean.

Life Under Feudalism

The feudal system had a **hierarchy**, or arrangement of people in order of power. At the top of the hierarchy was the king. Below the king was the **nobility**. The nobility were the nobles, or people who were of a high rank in society. Many nobles owned land. They also swore loyalty to the king. At the bottom of the hierarchy were **peasants**. These were poor people who farmed the land and lived on the manor in houses that had only one or two rooms. Peasants could not leave the manor unless the nobles allowed them to do so.

A system of **chivalry** developed in medieval times. Many rules were **formulated**, or developed, that explained how knights should behave. Knights were the soldiers who fought for the nobles. The rules of chivalry told the knight how to behave, how to be loyal, and how to be brave.

I've **formulated** a plan for us to go have some fun!

Sorry. I promised to mind my **manors**.

More New World History Words

chivalry

noun   the rules that knights were required to follow

hierarchy

noun   a way of organizing people into different levels of importance

nobility

noun   a group of people in society who have a high rank

peasant

noun   a person of lower rank that works on the land

Other Useful Words

formulate

verb   to plan or develop something

refute

verb   to prove that something or someone is wrong

Apply the Strategy

Look at a chapter in your textbook that your teacher identifies. Use definitions in the text to help you figure out the meaning of any new words you find.

The Right Word

Read each sentence. Look at the word or phrase that is underlined. Write a word from the box that means the same or almost the same as the underlined part of the sentence. Discuss your answers with a partner.

| chivalry | feudalism | heretics | hierarchy |
| manors | medieval | nobility | peasant |

1 _____ <u>A system in which people lived and worked on manors</u> was common during the Middle Ages.

2 _____ A <u>low ranking person who worked on the land</u> would have worked for the nobility.

3 _____ The wealthy landowners lived in <u>large houses with several smaller buildings around them</u>.

4 _____ In the Middle Ages, <u>people who disagreed with accepted beliefs</u> were punished by the church.

5 _____ The <u>high-ranking people</u> were often wealthy landowners.

6 _____ Feudalism and knighthood were part of <u>Middle Ages</u> Europe.

7 _____ Knights were bound to a certain behavior by <u>a code of rules</u>.

8 _____ Social life in England in the Middle Ages followed a strict <u>method of organizing people into different levels of importance</u>.

Word Challenge: Which Word?

With a partner, take turns saying the words listed below. Together, think of a statement for each one that gives a clue about its meaning. Write your statement next to the word. The first one has been done for you.

1 nobility _"We're second only to the king in society."_

2 formulate _____

3 chivalry _____

4 heretic _____

Word Challenge: What's Your Answer?

Take turns with a partner reading each question out loud and writing an answer on the line. Answer the questions with complete sentences. The first one has been done for you.

1 The man was accused of being a **heretic**. How do you think people felt about him? _They probably feared him._

2 What might the life of a **peasant** have been like during the Middle Ages? _____
_____

3 Who might own a **manor**? _____
_____

4 Why might someone **refute** a news report? _____
_____

Extend the Meaning

Write the letter of the word or phrase that best completes the sentence. Discuss your choices with a partner.

1 **Feudalism** is a system related to _____.

    a. banking

    b. land

    c. wars

2 **Chivalry** is a set of rules for _____.

    a. landowners

    b. knights

    c. peasants

3 The **hierarchy** told who was most _____.

    a. knowledgeable

    b. important

    c. brave

4 Medieval is a term that relates to a period of time in _____.

    a. Asia

    b. America

    c. Europe

Word Study: The Suffixes -er and -est

When the suffixes -er and -est are added to a root adjective such as *noble*, they change the adjectives meaning and use.

- The suffix -er is used to compare two things: *noble, nobler*.
- The suffix -est is used to compare three or more things: *noble, nobler, noblest*.

noble (adj.) righteous
nobler (adj.) more righteous
noblest (adj.) most righteous

A. Add -er and -est to the words below. Use a dictionary to check your spelling.

Root Adjective	Comparative Adjective (+ -er)	Superlative Adjective (+ -est)
1 fine		
2 rich		
3 sharp		

B. Tell whether the sentence is comparing two things or three or more things.

1 The comb was the finest she'd ever seen. _____

2 The chocolate cake was richer than the banana cake. _____

3 She chose the sharpest of the four pencils to write her essay. _____

The Language of Testing

How would you answer a question like this on a test?

What is a **characteristic** of a heretic?

    A. His or her beliefs are different from most.
    B. He or she refuses to fight in a war.
    C. He or she has a lot of money and power.
    D. He or she is paid to give advice.

 Tip

A *characteristic* of a thing is something it usually has or does.

Test Strategy: If you see a question that asks for a *characteristic* of something, rewrite it to ask for the thing that is true about something.

1   How could you say the question above in a different way?

_____

_____

Try the strategy again by asking these questions in a different way.

2   What is a characteristic of a peasant?

    A. He or she works on the land.
    B. He or she works in a store.
    C. He or she works on a ship.
    D. He or she works in a factory.

3   A characteristic of a feudal hierarchy is that

    A. some people behave in ways that go against society.
    B. knights have to follow a set of rules.
    C. some people work on the land.
    D. nobles are more important than peasants.

_____   _____

_____   _____

_____   _____

In Your Vocabulary Journal

Find each of these words in your World History Vocabulary Journal. Working by yourself or with a partner, use the definitions from pages 20 and 21 of your Work Text to complete the rest of the entry for each word.

chivalry	**feudalism**	**formulate**	**heretic**	**hierarchy**
manor	**medieval**	**nobility**	**peasant**	**refute**

Read the passage below. Think about the meanings of the new words printed in **bold**. Circle any synonyms for the new words. Draw an arrow from each synonym to the new word it describes. The first one has been done for you.

The Crusades Change Europe

Vocabulary Strategy

Look for synonyms to help you figure out the meaning of new words. Look for clues like *or* to help you find synonyms in a text.

In 1095, Pope Urban II wanted to win control of the Holy Land from the ruling Turks. He especially wanted to gain control of Jerusalem. Jerusalem is now the capital of Israel. He called for a **Crusade**, or a war to win control of the Holy Land. Thousands of people joined the battle for the Holy Land. In 1097, the first army of Crusaders left Europe. Their goal was the **conquest** of all of the Holy Land. There were many Crusades during the next 200 years.

The Crusaders only won control of the Holy Land for a short time, but they brought changes to Europe. One change was that money became more important. Before the Crusades, the **barter** system was often used instead of money. When people bartered, they exchanged one kind of good for another. As the Crusades increased trade between Europe and Asia, however, money became a better way to pay for goods.

Learning also became more important. Europeans learned more about eastern cultures. Some **scholars** studied the works of ancient Greek philosophers. They **rephrased** these works into a variety of modern languages so other scholars could read them.

New World History Words

barter
verb to trade goods for other goods

conquest
noun the act of taking over a country or group of people

crusade
noun a long effort to achieve something for a cause
verb to fight hard to achieve something for a cause

scholar
noun a person who studies a subject and knows a great deal about it

Now read the passage below and practice the strategy again. Underline any synonyms that will help you figure out the meanings of the new words.

Other Changes during the Middle Ages

During the Middle Ages, **guilds** became important in Europe. A guild was an organization of workers who had the same kind of business or trade. Some of the guilds were for bakers and glassmakers. The guilds made rules about prices and salaries.

A person who wanted to learn a trade would start by becoming an **apprentice**. An apprentice learned a trade by living and working with a master of that trade for a number of years. For example, a baker's apprentice would learn to bake bread.

The Middle Ages also brought years of a terrible illness called the **plague** to Europe and to Asia. The disease spread quickly from one person to another. The plague killed more than 23 million people in Europe.

At the end of the Middle Ages, some people were not happy with the Catholic Church. They **reacted** by starting different churches. These churches became the first Protestant churches. Some of the Protestant leaders believed that the best government should be a **theocracy**. In a theocracy, religious leaders control the government and make the laws.

More New World History Words

apprentice

noun   a young person who works for no pay to learn a skill

guild

noun   an organization of people who do the same job or work at the same skill

plague

noun   a deadly disease that spreads very quickly

theocracy

noun   a society that is ruled by a religious figure.

If you want to be my **apprentice**, you must speak the language of my **guild**.

Could you **rephrase** that?

Other Useful Words

react

verb   to respond in a certain way because of something that has happened to you

rephrase

verb   to say something in a different way

Apply the Strategy

Look at a chapter in your textbook that your teacher identifies. Find synonyms in the text to help you figure out the meaning of any new words you find.

Find the Word

Write a word from the box next to each clue. Then write the word formed by the boxed letters to finish the sentence below.

conquest	apprentice	guild	barter
theocracy	crusade	scholar	

1 a group of people who do the same work   __ __ __ __ ▢

2 a young person who works to learn a skill   __ __ __ __ __ ▢ __ __ __

3 the act of taking over a country   __ __ __ __ __ __ ▢ __

4 a long effort for a cause   __ __ __ __ __ __ ▢

5 a society ruled by a religious figure   __ __ __ __ __ __ ▢ __ __

6 a person who knows a lot about a subject   ▢ __ __ __ __ __ __

7 to trade goods for other goods   __ __ __ __ ▢ __

The **plague** is a deadly ___ ___ ___ ___ ___ ___ ___.

28

Word Challenge: Quick Pick

Read each question with a partner or by yourself. Think of a response and write it on the line. Explain your answer.

1 Which is a **conquest**: winning a sports game or taking over a country? _Taking over a_ _country is a conquest._

2 Is a society ruled by a religious figure a **theocracy** or an autocracy?_____
_____

3 Is a **guild** a group of people who are from the same family or who do the same job? _____
_____

4 Which would be of more interest to a **scholar**: a library or a sports field? _____
_____

Word Challenge: What's Your Answer?

Take turns with a partner reading each question out loud and writing an answer. Answer each question in a complete sentence. The first one has been done for you.

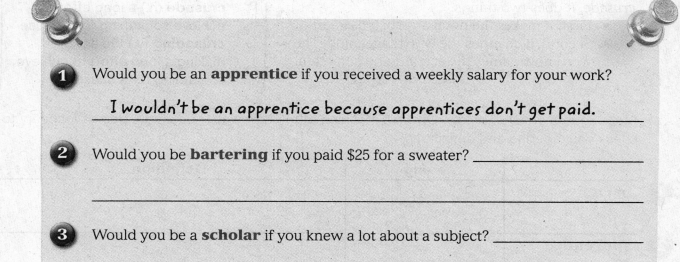

1 Would you be an **apprentice** if you received a weekly salary for your work?

I wouldn't be an apprentice because apprentices don't get paid.

2 Would you be **bartering** if you paid $25 for a sweater? _____
_____

3 Would you be a **scholar** if you knew a lot about a subject? _____
_____

4 If someone you knew had the **plague**, what would you do? _____
_____

Analogies

Use a word from the box to finish each sentence. Write the word on the line. Discuss your answers with a partner.

apprentice	barter	plague	theocracy

1 Master is to _____ as teacher is to student.

2 Religious leader is to _____ as president is to democracy.

3 Deadly is to _____ as smelly is to garbage.

4 Trade is to _____ as revise is to change.

Word Study: The -ing Ending

When the -ing ending is added to a noun such as *crusade*, it does two things:

- First, it makes the noun a verb: *crusading*.
- Second, it changes the word's meaning. The word now names the act of doing something.

> Drop the -e from the end of a word before adding -ing.
>
> **crusade** (n.) a long effort to achieve something for a cause
> **crusading** (v.) the act of making a long effort to achieve something for a cause

Add -ing to the words below. Give the meaning of the new word you made. Use a dictionary to check your spelling and definitions.

		+ -ing	Definition
1	barter		
2	apprentice		
3	react		
4	rephrase		

The Language of Testing

How would you answer a question like this on a test?

What is (**the main purpose of**) a *crusade*?

- A. to learn a new trade
- B. to meet new people
- C. to achieve something for a cause
- D. to visit a new place and learn about the people

> 💡 **Tip**
>
> The word *purpose* can mean *reason* or *use*. The word *main* means *most important*.

Test Strategy: If you see a question that uses the word *purpose*, rewrite it using the word *reason*, *function*, or *use*. If the question also includes the word *main*, look for the most important reason or use.

1 How could you say the question above in a different way?

_____

_____

Try the strategy again by asking these questions in a different way.

2 What is the main purpose of a conquest?

- A. to take over a group of people
- B. to achieve something important
- C. to learn about a group of people
- D. to stop migration

_____

_____

3 For what purpose might someone hire an apprentice?

- A. to get an expert employee
- B. to teach someone new a craft
- C. to learn something new
- D. to get an employee to train others

_____

_____

In Your Vocabulary Journal

Find each of these words in your World History Vocabulary Journal. Working by yourself or with a partner, use the definitions from pages 26 and 27 of your Work Text to complete the rest of the entry for each word.

apprentice	**barter**	**conquest**	**crusade**	**guild**
plague	**react**	**rephrase**	**scholar**	**theocracy**

Lesson 6 Trade and Exploration

Read the passage below. Think about the meaning of the words printed in **bold**. Circle any words that end with *-al*, *-ize*, or *-tion*. Write what you think the word means next to it. Remember that *-al* means "related to", *-ize* means "to make" and *-tion* names a process. The first one has been done for you.

The Commercial Revolution

Vocabulary Strategy

Use familiar prefixes and suffixes to help you understand the meanings of new words.

related to trade

During the 1300s, there were many changes in the way business was done in Europe. The many **commercial** changes, or business changes, were called the Commercial Revolution.

We can **generalize** about many things of this period. To generalize about the Commercial Revolution, we must say that trade grew both between the countries of Europe and with other parts of the world. New **commodities**, or products, like silks and spices were brought to Europe from Asia. New trade routes developed, banking became important, and **navigation**, or planning a course for travel, improved.

An instrument called the **compass** improved navigation. The compass was invented in China. It uses a magnet to point out the directions north, south, east, and west. By using a compass, sailors could sail far from land with less chance of getting lost at sea.

New World History Words

commercial
  adjective   done for a profit

commodity
  noun   something that is sold or traded

compass
  noun   a tool that is used for finding directions

navigation
  noun   the process of planning a course for travel

Now read the passage below and practice the vocabulary strategy again. Underline two words printed in **bold** that end in *-ism*. Remember that *-ism* names a belief. Write what you think each word means near it.

A Changing World

The growth of trade between Europe and other parts of the world brought new ideas to Europe. The years from 1400 to 1700 were called the **Renaissance**, which means rebirth. This was a period of new ideas and learning.

England, Spain, and France followed a theory called **mercantilism**. According to this theory, a nation needs large amounts of gold and silver to be wealthy and strong. Nations would become wealthy by selling more goods to other countries than they bought. Nations put **tariffs**, or taxes, on goods from other countries to prevent people from buying them.

During the 1500s, Europeans began trading in Japan. The leaders of Japan, however, started a policy of **isolationism** to keep Japan apart from other countries. We can **infer** that the Japanese leaders wanted to keep their own laws and customs. Isolationism lasted more than 200 years in Japan.

More New World History Words

isolationism

noun   a policy of avoiding contact with other countries

mercantilism

noun   a policy of building wealth through trade

renaissance

noun   a period of time during which there is a growth in learning and the arts, or the period in Europe from 1400 to 1700

tariff

noun   a tax that the government collects on imported goods

My **navigation** skills are terrible! We will be lost.

We can't get lost with this **compass**!

Other Useful Words

generalize

verb   to say something that is almost always true, or to leave out the details

infer

verb   to come to a conclusion

Apply the Strategy

Look at a chapter in your textbook that your teacher indentifies. Use prefixes and suffixes to help you figure out the meaning of new words.

Categories

Write the words from the word bank in the correct boxes below. Some words may be used in more than one box. Discuss your choices with a partner.

commercialism	commodity	compass
isolationism	mercantilism	navigation	tariff

Trade	Travel

34

Word Challenge: Quick Pick

Read each question with a partner or by yourself. Think of a response and write it on the line. Explain your answer.

1 Would a country with a policy of mercantilism trade with other countries or do battle with them? _They would trade with other countries._

2 Is a country with closed borders **commercial**, or are they practicing **isolationism**? _____
_____

3 Does **navigation** involve travel or shopping? _____
_____

4 What would show a **renaissance** has happened: more art or more people? _____
_____

Word Challenge: Correct or Incorrect

Take turns with a partner reading the sentences below out loud. Write **C** if the sentence is correct, and write **I** if the sentence is incorrect. Rewrite the incorrect sentences. The first one has been done for you.

1 _C_ The government collected a **tariff** on lamb from New Zealand.

2 _____ The cyclists used a **compass** to determine how far they had traveled.
_____

3 _____ For our new business, we decided cell phones were a **commodity** that would sell well.
_____

4 _____ Lee **inferred** from the empty plate and the paw prints that his dog had eaten his sandwich.
_____

Synonyms

In each of the groups, circle the synonyms. Discuss your choices with a partner.

1
commodity	tariff
sale	product

2
tariff	exchange
tax	good

3
exchange	trade
purchase	commodity

4
navigation	course-plotting
compass	profit-making

Word Study: The Suffix -ion

When the suffix -ion is added to a verb such as navigate, it does two things:

- First, it changes the verb to a noun: navigation.
- Second, it changes the word's meaning. The new word names a process or result.

Drop the -e from the end of a word before adding -ion.

navigate (v.) to steer or plot a course
navigation (n.) the process of planning a course of travel

Add the suffix -ion to each root verb to make a new word. Then, write the definition of the new word. Use a dictionary to check your spelling and definitions.

	+ -ion	Definition
1 isolate		
2 imitate		
3 reject		

The Language of Testing

How would you answer a question like this on a test?

For many years, the Chinese government practiced isolationism. What does this **suggest** about the Chinese government?

Tip

When the word *suggest* is used in a question, you should draw a conclusion about information in the question.

    A. It did not want relations with other countries.
    B. It wanted to become rich from trade.
    C. It was interested in exploration.
    D. It valued profit over all else.

Test Strategy: If you see a question that uses the word *suggest*, rewrite it so that it asks you what the information probably means or what your conclusion is.

1 How could you say the question above in a different way?

_____

_____

Try the strategy again by asking these questions in a different way.

2 What does it suggest about a group of travelers if they pull out a compass?

    A. They need to know the time.
    B. They need directions.
    C. They need to know how much further they have to go.
    D. They want to know how fast they're traveling.

3 What does it suggest if a business is required to pay a tariff?

    A. It has sold goods to another country.
    B. It has made a large profit.
    C. It has exchanged goods with another business.
    D. It has purchased goods from another country.

_____

_____

_____

_____

In Your Vocabulary Journal

Find each of these words in your World History Vocabulary Journal. Working by yourself or with a partner, use the definitions from pages 32 and 33 of your Work Text to complete the rest of the entry for each word.

commercial	commodity	compass	generalize	infer
isolationism	mercantilism	navigation	renaissance	tariff

Lesson 7 Absolutism

Read the passage below. Think about the meanings of the new words printed in **bold**. Underline any familiar root words within some of the new words that might help you figure out what these words mean. Write what the root means near the word. The first one has been done for you.

monarch=king

Absolute Monarchies

Vocabulary Strategy

Use words you know to help unlock the meaning of unfamiliar words in the same family. For example, *settle* can help you unlock the meaning of *settlement*, *settler*, and *unsettled*. You can keep track of these word groups by making a Word Web.

In the 1400s, some nations in Europe were **monarchies**. A monarchy is a government that is ruled by a king or queen. Sometimes a king or queen is called a **sovereign**.

France, Spain, and Russia were three nations that had monarchs who believed in **absolutism**. Under absolutism, the king had absolute, or total power to make all laws and decisions for the country. The king could decide by himself to raise taxes or to go to war against another country. Many absolute monarchs believed that God gave them the power to make all laws.

Total control of a country by a leader is also called **despotism**. It is a **fallacy**, or false idea, to think that all despots were bad leaders, however. Some of these leaders in the late 1700s made good laws to improve their countries. However, many despots were very cruel.

King Louis XIV of France

 New World History Words

absolutism
noun a system in which one ruler has total power over a country

despotism
noun cruel and unfair government by very powerful rulers

monarchy
noun a country that is ruled by a king or queen

sovereign
adjective to have the most power, or to be independent, especially in the case of a country
noun a royal ruler of a country

38

Now read this passage and practice the vocabulary strategy again. Circle familiar root words that are found in larger, unfamiliar words. Write the meaning of each circled root word near it.

A Different Kind of Monarchy

England also had a monarchy, but it was not an absolute monarchy. Starting in 1295, England had a group of lawmakers called **Parliament**. As time passed, Parliament had more and more power and the kings had less power. Today, a Queen still **reigns**, or rules, England, but all laws are made by Parliament.

From 1642 to 1660, there was no monarchy in England. Instead, a dictator named Oliver Cromwell ruled. After his death, a king began to rule England again. This period of time was called the **Restoration**.

Diplomacy also began in Europe in the 1400s. Diplomacy means representatives of nations work together to solve problems and create treaties. The job of the representatives is to **articulate**, or explain clearly, what their nation wants.

More New World History Words

diplomacy

noun   the process of developing good relationships between countries

parliament

noun   a group of people in some countries who make the laws

reign

verb   to rule or have power, especially over a country

noun   the period of time during which someone or a group rules

restoration

noun   the process of bringing something back or making something like new

Other Useful Words

articulate

verb   to express thoughts clearly and easily

fallacy

noun   a false or mistaken idea

Apply the Strategy

Look at a chapter in your textbook that your teacher identifies. Use familiar root words to help you figure out the meaning of any new words you find.

The Right Word

Read each sentence. Look at the word or phrase that is underlined. Write a word from the box that means the same or almost the same as the underlined part of the sentence. Discuss your answers with a partner.

monarchy	despotism	diplomacy	reign
sovereign	absolutism	restoration	parliament

1 _____ The queen is expected to <u>rule over the country</u> for many years to come.

2 _____ In New Zealand, the <u>group of people who make the laws</u> works in a building shaped like a beehive.

3 _____ After many years in a dusty basement, the painting required <u>the process of making something like new.</u>

4 _____ Ambassadors from many countries in the world are chosen to perform <u>the job of maintaining good relations between countries.</u>

5 _____ Denmark has been a <u>country ruled by a king or queen</u> for more than one thousand years.

6 _____ The fascist leaders of World War II were known for their <u>cruel leadership.</u>

7 _____ The ideals of democracy do not allow for <u>a system in which one leader rules a country with total power.</u>

8 _____ After many years of British rule, India became <u>independent</u> in 1947.

Word Challenge: Which Word?

With a partner, take turns saying the words listed below. Together, think of a statement for each one that gives a clue about its meaning. Write your statement next to the word. The first one has been done for you.

1 absolutism *"I'm a government with one ruler!"*

2 articulate _____

3 fallacy _____

4 reign _____

Word Challenge: Finish the Idea

With a partner, take turns reading the incomplete sentences below. Write an ending for each. The first one has been done for you.

1 The people fought for the **restoration** of the building because _____
it was falling apart.
_____

2 **Diplomacy** is important because _____
_____

3 Countries should fight **despotism** because _____
_____

4 England is a **monarchy** because _____
_____

Extend the Meaning

Write the letter of the word or phrase that best completes the sentence. Discuss your choices with a partner.

1 A _____ might **reign** over a coutry.

    a. shopkeeper

    b. leader

    c. public servant

3 A **sovereign** might _____.

    a. rule from a royal court

    b. be an assistant to a royal

    c. make clothes for royalty

2 A **restoration** might involve _____.

    a. tearing down an old house

    b. fixing up an old house

    c. buying a new house

4 **Diplomacy** might include _____.

    a. going to war

    b. finding the middle ground

    c. terrorizing innocent people

Word Study: The Suffix -ism

When the suffix -*ism* is added to a noun, such as *despot*, it changes the noun's meaning. The suffix -*ism* can express a belief, process, or practice. The word now refers to a belief or practice: *despotism*.

despot (n.) a powerful ruler who rules cruelly and unfairly
despotism (n.) cruel and unfair government by powerful rulers

Write a definition for the root words below. Then, add -*ism* to the words. If necessary, drop the -*e* from words before adding -*ism*. Use a dictionary to check your spelling and definitions.

	Root Word	Definition	+ -*ism*
1	absolute		
2	feudal		
3	isolation		
4	mercantile		

The Language of Testing

How would you answer a question like this on a test?

Which of the following **compares closely to** despotism?

    A. autocracy
    B. democracy
    C. communism
    D. socialism

💡 **Tip**

The phrase *compares closely to* means *is most like.*

Test Strategy: If you see the phrase *compares closely to* on a test, rewrite it using the phrase *is most like.*

1 How could you say the question above in a different way?

_____

_____

Try the strategy again by asking these questions in a different way.

2 All of the following compare closely to the meaning of *restoration* except

    A. restore
    B. abolition
    C. reinstate
    D. return

_____

_____

3 What word compares closely to the meaning of *diplomacy*?

    A. invasion
    B. negotiation
    C. cooperation
    D. compromise

_____

_____

_____

In Your Vocabulary Journal

Find each of these words in your World History Vocabulary Journal. Working by yourself or with a partner, use the definitions from pages 38 and 39 of your Work Text to complete the rest of the entry for each word.

absolutism	**articulate**	**despotism**	**diplomacy**	**fallacy**
monarchy	**parliament**	**reign**	**restoration**	**sovereign**

Expansion and Imperialism

Read the passage below. Think about the meaning of the words in **bold**. Underline any familiar root words within some of the new words to help you figure out what these words mean. Write the meaning of the root word near the word in the passage. The first one has been done for you.

Empires and Colonies

to grow

Vocabulary Strategy

Use words you know to help unlock the meaning of unfamiliar words in the same family. For example, *expand* can help you unlock the meaning of *expansion*.

About the year 1300, Muslims won control of many parts of Asia, Africa, and the Middle East. Muslims follow the religion of Islam. The **expansion**, or growth, of Muslim empires brought Islam to many parts of the world.

At the end of the 1400s, explorers discovered new trade routes to Asia. In the 1600s, England gained control of **territory**, or land, in India.

Christopher Columbus was an explorer who sailed for Spain. His **strategy**, or plan, was to reach Asia by sailing west across the Atlantic Ocean. Instead of reaching Asia, however, Columbus reached the Americas in 1492. The Americas were a new world to Europeans.

For many years, Spain, Britain, and France ruled **colonies** in the Americas. A colony is a country that is controlled by another nation. The Spanish wanted to teach the Catholic religion to the Native Americans in their colonies. The Spanish built many missions and sent **missionaries** to teach religion to the Native Americans.

New World History Words

colony

noun a settlement or land that belongs to another country

expansion

noun the act of becoming greater in size or amount

missionary

noun a person sent to a foreign place to teach about his or her religion

territory

noun land controlled by a country or ruler

Now read the passage below and practice the vocabulary strategy again. Underline any familiar words that are found in larger unfamiliar words. Write what these words mean near them in the passage.

Building Empires

During the 1600s and 1700s, England, Spain and France won control of colonies in America. There was **rivalry**, or competition, between England and France to control the most colonies in America.

Many years later, between 1850 and 1914, **imperialism** became important in Europe. Imperialism means a nation takes control of colonies to build an empire. England ruled many colonies and had the world's largest empire.

Assimilation often took place in a colony. Some people in the colony took on the culture of the ruling nation. However, as colonists built their lives in other lands, their loyalties shifted to their new homes. They didn't want to be ruled by the old country anymore, but wanted to make the colonies into a new country. **Nationalism**, or a strong love and loyalty that people have for their own country, made them want to separate from the old country. Back home, however, the **perspective** was different. Owning colonies made the people in the old country feel powerful.

More New World History Words

assimilation

noun   the act of learning or adopting the ideas, customs, and lifestyles of another culture

imperialism

noun   a system in which a rich and powerful country has control over other countries

nationalism

noun   strong feelings of loyalty to one's country

rivalry

noun   competition or fighting

Other Useful Words

perspective

noun   a specific way of thinking about something

strategy

noun   a plan for reaching a goal

This **rivalry** for colonies is really getting out of hand!

Apply the Strategy

Look at a chapter in your textbook that your teacher identifies. Use familiar root words to help you figure out the meaning of new words you find.

Find the Word

Write a word from the box next to each clue. Then write the word formed by the boxed letters to complete the sentence below.

territory	assimilation	imperialism	colony
missionary	expansion	nationalism	

1. when one country controls others   __ __ __ [ ] __ __ __ __ __ __ __

2. a country or region controlled by another   __ __ __ __ __ [ ] __

3. getting bigger   [ ] __ __ __ __ __ __ __

4. a religious teacher   [ ] __ __ __ __ __ __ __ __

5. loyalty to one's country   __ __ __ [ ] __ __ __ __ __ __

6. land controlled by a country or ruler   __ __ [ ] __ __ __ __ __ __

7. adopting new customs   __ [ ] __ __ __ __ __ __ __ __ __

People involved in a **rivalry** are often called __ __ __ __ __ __ .

Word Challenge: What's Your Answer

Take turns with a partner reading each question out loud and writing an answer on the line. Answer the questions in complete sentences. The first one has been done for you.

1 What reason could you give for being against **imperialism**? _A stronger country_ _can take advantage of a weaker country under imperialism._

2 How would you feel if your country was a **colony** of another country? _____ _____

3 How might you change if you faced **assimilation** in another country? _____ _____

4 What **rivalry** are you involved with at school? _____ _____

Word Challenge: Finish the Idea

With a partner, take turns reading the incomplete sentences below. Write an ending for each. The first one has been done for you.

1 A student needs a **strategy** for studying for a test because _he or she_ _might not study what is important._

2 I have a different **perspective** from my friend about the best sneakers because _____ _____

3 **Missionaries** went to the new world because _____ _____

4 **Nationalism** can lead to war because _____ _____

Synonyms and Antonyms

Write either a synonym or an antonym for the vocabulary words below. In some cases, you might be able to provide both. Discuss your answers with a partner.

		Synonym	Antonym
1	assimilation		
2	colony		
3	expansion		
4	nationalism		
5	rivalry		

Word Study: The Suffix *-ion*

When the suffix *-ion* is added to a verb such as *assimilate*, it does two things:

- First, it makes a noun: *assimilation*.
- Second, the word now names a process.

Drop the *-e* from the end of the word before adding *-ion*.

assimilate (v.) to learn or adopt new customs
assimilation (n.) the act of learning or adopting new customs

Add the suffix *-ion* to each root verb to make a new word. Write a definition for each. Use a dictionary to check your spelling and your definitions.

		+ *-ion*	Definition
1	vibrate		
2	migrate		
3	vacate		
4	imitate		

The Language of Testing

How would you answer a question like this on a test?

What is a **characteristic** of a colony?

    A. It rules other countries.
    B. It is under the control of another country.
    C. It has complete political independence.
    D. It is always ruled by a king or queen.

 Tip

A *characteristic* of a thing is something that it usually has or does.

Test Strategy: If you see a question that uses the word *characteristic*, rewrite it to ask for the thing that is true about the subject of the question.

1 How could you say the question above in a different way?

_____

_____

Try the strategy again by asking these questions in a different way.

2 What is a characteristic of missionaries?

    A. They are powerful rulers.
    B. They are Christian teachers.
    C. They are fierce competitors.
    D. They are proud citizens.

3 What is a characteristic of nationalism?

    A. pride in one's country
    B. a desire to rule other countries
    C. learning new customs
    D. growing larger in size or amount

_____   _____

_____   _____

_____   _____

In Your Vocabulary Journal

Find each of these words in your World History Vocabulary Journal. Working by yourself or with a partner, use the definitions from pages 44 and 45 of your Work Text to complete the rest of the entry for each word.

assimilation	colony	expansion	imperialism	missionary
nationalism	perspective	rivalry	strategy	territory

Revolution and Change

Read the passage below. Think about the meaning of the new words printed in **bold**. Underline any words or phrases that contrast a word you know with a new word or idea. The first one has been done for you.

The French Revolution

Vocabulary Strategy

Use contrasts to help you understand the meanings of new words. Look for clues that point out contrasts, such as *unlike*, *instead*, or *different from*.

A period called the **Enlightenment** took place during the 1600s and 1700s. The leaders of this period turned to <u>science and reason rather than tradition and religion</u> to solve problems. Unlike leaders of the past, they believed all people had the natural right to freedom. These ideas helped Americans win a war for freedom from Great Britain.

The French wanted more freedom, too. In 1789, the French Revolution began. France's king, Louis XVI, asked other countries to fight against the leaders of the French Revolution. The king had worked against the government, so he was found guilty of **treason** and killed.

In 1789, some French leaders were **moderates**. Unlike the **radicals**, they wanted to make some changes, but not too many, to improve the government. However, the radical leaders won control of the government.

These radicals completely changed the laws and government. The radicals said they believed in the ideas of the French Revolution. Two of those ideas were liberty and equality. The actions of the radicals **contradicted** these ideas, however. They had thousands of people killed for disagreeing with their ideas.

✔ New World History Words

enlightenment

noun   the act of giving or gaining knowledge about something, or the movement in the 18th century based on science and reason

moderate

adjective   avoiding extreme behavior or beliefs

noun   someone who avoids extreme behavior or beliefs

radical

adjective   showing extreme beliefs

noun   someone who has extreme beliefs

treason

noun   an action carried out to harm one's own country

Now read the passage below and practice the strategy again. Underline any words or phrases that contrast something you know with a new word or idea. Look for clues that point out contrasts, like *unlike*, *instead*, or *different from*.

After the French Revolution

In 1789, Napoleon Bonaparte, a French army leader, became the ruler of France. Napoleon's army conquered many countries in Europe, and he chose new leaders for these countries. He was defeated in 1815.

In 1814, the leaders of France, England, Austria and two other nations met in Vienna, Austria. Their meetings were called the Congress of Vienna. The meetings were **counterrevolutionary**. Their goal was to end all governments that had been started by the French Revolution and Napoleon.

The leader of the Congress of Vienna was Prince Metternich. He was **characterized** as a person who wanted a lot of power. Unlike a radical, who wants change, he was a **conservative**. He did not agree with French Revolution ideas about freedom and equality.

The leaders in Vienna shared Metternich's ideas. They were **reactionaries**. Unlike revolutionaries, they wanted to make Europe the way it had been before 1789. In addition, they wanted to stop future revolutions. These leaders were also **royalists**. They did not want a democratic government, but instead planned to have their old kings and queens rule Europe again.

More New World History Words

conservative

noun　someone who resists change

adjective　resisting change

counterrevolutionary

adjective　about policies or people who want to reverse the effects of social or political change

reactionary

adjective　wanting to return to an older system

noun　a person who wants to return to an older system

royalist

noun　someone who supports rule by a king or queen

Other Useful Words

characterize

verb　to describe someone or something by a specific thing

contradict

verb　to go against or say the opposite of something

Congress of Vienna

Turning all clocks back won't **counter** the changes made by the **revolution**!

Apply the Strategy

Look at a chapter in your textbook that your teacher identifies. Use contrasts in the text to help you figure out the meaning of any new words you find.

Categories

Sort the words printed in **bold** into the correct boxes below. Some words can be sorted into more than one box. Discuss your answers with a partner.

conservative   **counterrevolutionary**   **characterize**   **contradict**   **radical**

moderate   **enlightenment**   **reactionary**   **royalist**   **treason**

Descriptions of Political Beliefs (adjectives)	Political and Cultural Beliefs (nouns)	Actions (verbs)
conservative		

52

Word Challenge: Would You/If You . . .

Take turns with a partner reading the following questions aloud. Write an answer for each on the lines. The first one has been done for you.

1 Would you want to change the rules if you were **conservative**? _No. If I was_ _conservative, I wouldn't want to change the rules._

2 Would you be committing **treason** if you joined the army? _____

_____

3 Would you become the best friend of a **radical** if you were a **reactionary**? _____

_____

4 Would you want to help a **counterrevolutionary** if you were a **moderate**? _____

_____

Word Challenge: Which Word?

With a partner or by yourself, take turns saying the words below. Together, think of a statement for each one that gives a clue about its meaning. Write your statement next to the word.

1 enlightenment _"I used science and reason to solve problems!"_

2 contradict _____

3 moderate _____

4 treason _____

5 reactionary _____

Extend the Meaning

Write the letter of the word or phrase that best completes each sentence. Discuss your answers with a partner.

1 A **royalist** wants a government with a _____.

    a. nomad

    b. scholar

    c. monarch

2 If you lived during the **Enlightenment**, you would try to solve problems using _____.

    a. science

    b. religion

    c. tradition

3 When you **contradict** your friend, you _____.

    a. make a statement that is the opposite of what your friend says

    b. eat a lot of cheese

    c. play baseball with friends

4 A **moderate** would want _____ in the government.

    a. no change

    b. some change

    c. many changes

Word Study: The Suffix -ment

When the suffix *-ment* is added to a verb such as *enlighten*, it does two things:

- First, it changes the word to a noun: *enlightenment*.
- Second, the word now names a state of being.

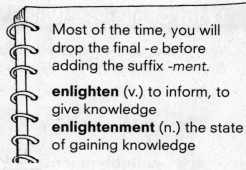

Most of the time, you will drop the final *-e* before adding the suffix *-ment*.

enlighten (v.) to inform, to give knowledge
enlightenment (n.) the state of gaining knowledge

Add the suffix *-ment* to the verbs below. Write a definition for each new word. Use a dictionary to check your spelling and definitions.

		+ -ment	Definition
1	judge		
2	acknowledge		
3	encourage		
4	enhance		

The Language of Testing

How would you answer a question like this on a test?

Which of the following is an example of treason?

A. stealing from the grocery store
B. lying to your mother or father
C. selling your government's secrets
D. cheating on a driver's license test

 Tip

If you see the words *which of the following* on a test, you have to choose one of the answers (A, B, C, or D) to answer the question.

Test Strategy: If a question has the phrase *which of the following* in it, you may want to ask the question in a different way. Start your restated question with *who*, *where*, or *what*.

1 How could you say the question above in a different way?

_____

_____

Try the strategy again by asking these questions in a different way.

2 Which of the following is true of royalists?

A. They are powerful rulers.
B. They support kings and queens.
C. They resist change.
D. They are kings and queens.

3 Which of the following people might be called conservative?

A. a man who always wears the same suit
B. a woman who travels to new places every year
C. a college student who attends three different schools
D. a person who has had many jobs

_____

_____

_____

_____

In Your Vocabulary Journal

Find each of these words in your World History Vocabulary Journal. Working by yourself or with a partner, use the definitions from pages 50 and 51 of your Work Text to complete the rest of the entry for each word.

characterize   conservative   contradict   counterrevolutionary

enlightenment   moderate   radical   reactionary   royalist   treason

Lesson 10
Industrialization and Economics

Read the passage below. Think about the meanings of the words in **bold**. Circle any words that end with *-ation*. Remember that *-ation* names a process. Write what you think each circled word means near it in the passage. The first one has been done for you.

Vocabulary Strategy

Use familiar suffixes to help you understand the meaning of new words.

The Industrial Revolution

The Industrial Revolution began in England during the 1700s. It is characterized by a change from making goods by hand at home to making goods by machines in factories.

The growth of factories brought about new processes as well. One new process was *become more industrial* (**industrialization**,)the development of many new industries that used machines. Some of the new industries made cloth, steel, and trains. Because of industrialization people moved to cities to work in factories.

Mechanization was another new process. Mechanization means that work is done by machines. If we try to **compile**, or put together, a list of machine made products, the list would be very, very long. Sewing, for example, was now done by machine instead of by hand.

The Industrial Revolution also brought about changes in business. After 1860, **corporations** were started as a new way to own businesses. A corporation is a business in which many people own shares, or part of the company. Some corporations became **monopolies**. A monopoly controls all production and sales for a product. The monopoly in the American steel industry controlled everything that involved steel for a number of years.

 New World History Words

corporation

noun a large business or company

industrialization

noun the development of many factories

mechanization

noun the process of using machines to do more tasks

monopoly

noun complete control of products or services by a company, person, or state

Now read the passage and practice the strategy again. Circle any words that end in *-ism*. Remember that *-ism* names a belief or a system. Write near each circled word what you think it means.

Economic Changes

The ideas of **capitalism** became important during the Industrial Revolution. Capitalism means people own their own businesses and keep the profits they earn. Business owners decide for themselves what they want to produce.

Industry growth sometimes caused **depressions**, periods in which business activity is very slow, causing many people to lose jobs and become poor.

Some people **critiqued**, or criticized, capitalism and said it allowed business owners to become rich while their workers were poor. Some people thought that **socialism** was better. Socialism is a system in which the government controls businesses and industries and all people are treated equally.

In 1848, Karl Marx wrote a book about **communism**. Under communism, the government owns land and businesses, and makes all of the decisions. Communist governments allow people very little freedom.

More New World History Words

capitalism

noun   system in which property, business, and industry are privately owned

communism

noun   a system in which the government controls all businesses and decides what factories and farmers will produce

depression

noun   a time of little economic activity, or a period of unemployment and poverty

socialism

noun   a system in which the government controls businesses and industries and all people are treated equally

"I love my **monopoly**. I control every steel **corporation**!"

Other Useful Words

compile

verb   to put together

critique

verb   to criticize or judge

Apply the Strategy

Look at a chapter in your textbook that your teacher identifies. Use prefixes and suffixes to help you figure out the meaning of new words.

Matching

Finish the sentences in Group A with words from Group B. Discuss your answers with a partner.

Group A

1. Many people work for a _____ that makes computers.

2. Miguel put together, or _____, a list of family and friends to invite to his graduation party.

3. The economic system that allows people to own their own businesses and keep the profits is _____.

4. The development of many new industries starting in the 1700s was called _____.

5. A business that has complete control over sales and production of a product is a _____.

Group B

A. capitalism

B. corporation

C. industrialization

D. monopoly

E. compiled

Group A

6. During the _____ of the 1930s, many people lost all their money on the stock market.

7. Nothing is considered personal property in the system of _____.

8. Government ownership of business and the use of profits for the good of the people is called _____.

9. The use of machines to do work that had been done by hand is _____.

10. When you examine, judge, and criticize something, you _____ it.

Group B

F. communism

G. depression

H. mechanization

I. critique

J. socialism

Word Challenge: Would You Rather . . .

Take turns with a partner reading the questions below out loud, think of a response, and write it on the line. Explain your answers. The first one has been done for you.

1 Would you rather **compile** or **critique** recipes for a class cookbook? _I would like to_ _critique recipes because I am a good cook._

2 Would you rather live during a **depression** or the early days of **industrialization**? _____ _____

3 Would you rather live without **mechanization** or **corporations**? _____ _____

4 Would you rather live under the system of **socialism** or **capitalism**? _____ _____

Word Challenge: Correct or Incorrect

Take turns with a partner reading each sentence aloud. Write **C** if the sentence is correct. Write **I** if it is not. Rewrite the incorrect sentences. The first one has been done for you.

1 __I__ **Industrialization** means to make products at home by hand.

Industrialization means the development of new industries that use machines.

2 _____ People buy shares in a **corporation**.

_____

3 _____ **Capitalism** is a system that allows private ownership of businesses.

_____

4 _____ The government owns businesses and uses profits for the good of the people under **socialism**.

_____

Extend the Meaning

Write the letter of the word or phrase that best completes each sentence. Discuss your answers with a partner.

1 _____ during a **depression**.
   a. People become wealthy
   b. People lose jobs
   c. More people travel

2 **Industrialization** would cause the development of _____.
   a. many jobs that can be done in school
   b. many new farms
   c. new industries that use machines

3 You might wish to **compile** _____.
   a. information from three books for a report
   b. a warm pair of winter boots
   c. a new baseball hat

4 You can **critique** _____.
   a. a new book or TV show
   b. the ocean
   c. an apprentice

Word Study: The Suffix -ization

When the suffix *-ization* is added to an adjective, it does two things:
- First, it changes the adjective to a noun: *industrialization*.
- Second, it changes the word's meaning. The word now names a process or result of something.

industrial (adj.) relating to industries or business
industrialization (n.) the process of developing many industries or businesses

Underline the root word in each *-ization* word. Write a definition of each root word.

1 industrialization _____

2 civilization _____

3 metropolitanization _____

4 socialization _____

5 mechanization _____

60

The Language of Testing

How would you answer a question like this on a test?

Each of the following statements is true

except

A. Capitalism involves private ownership.
B. Communism involves ownership by the community.
C. Socialism involves ownership by socialites.
D. A monopoly involves complete control of something.

 Tip

The word *except* means you should look for something that means the opposite of the word or phrase before *except*. The opposite of true is false. So in this question, you should look for the answer that is false.

Test Strategy: Make sure you understand the question. Read it carefully. Then, if it has the word *except* in it, ask the question in a different way. Remember that you are looking for the statement that is false.

1 How could you say the question above in a different way?

_____

_____

Try the strategy again by asking these questions in a different way.

2 All of these are a corporations except

A. a small flower store
B. a multi-million dollar oil company
C. an ice cream maker with stores in every state
D. a chain of bookstores

_____

_____

3 All of these are generally results of a depression except

A. unemployment
B. poverty
C. loss
D. new jobs

_____

_____

In Your Vocabulary Journal

Find each of these words in your World History Vocabulary Journal. Working by yourself or with a partner, use the definitions from pages 56 and 57 of your Work Text to complete the rest of the entry for each word.

capitalism   **communism**   **compile**   **corporation**   **critique**

depression   **industrialization**   **mechanization**   **monopoly**   **socialism**

Social Issues and Reform

Read the passage below. Think about the meanings of the words in **bold**. Create associations between familiar words and ideas and the new words to help you anchor the meaning of the new words. The first one has been done for you.

Reform for Workers

Vocabulary Strategy

Create associations between familiar words and ideas with the new words to help you "anchor" the meaning of new words. You can use a Word Anchor to help you create associations.

After the Industrial Revolution began, many people became factory workers. People who did factory work were referred to as (labor). *work*

One labor problem in the 1800s was that young children were factory workers. Try to **visualize**, or see a picture in your mind, of five year old children working in factories. People in England and America began working for **reform**, or improvements in factories to solve this problem.

In America in the late 1800s, people who worked for reform were called **progressives**. As time passed, the progressives passed new labor laws to help workers.

Workers also helped themselves by starting labor unions. Unions were groups of workers that worked with labor leaders to get better working conditions. Labor leaders told factory owners about the changes they wanted. If factory owners refused to listen to labor leaders, the leaders could start a **strike**. A strike is a decision by labor to stop working in order to get better treatment from factory owners. Strikes can help workers win more money and better working conditions. Another way for people to fight against bad treatment was to stage a rebellion, or **uprising**.

New World History Words

labor

noun   work, or the people working in a factory

progressive

noun   someone who wants to improve society

reform

noun   an improvement in a law, social system, or institution

verb   to improve a law, social system, or institution

strike

verb   to stop working until you get better working conditions or pay

uprising

noun   an act of rebellion, often violent

Now read the passage below and practice the strategy again. Write near the new words any associations you have that will help you anchor their meaning.

Other Changes and Reforms

Many people in Europe were very poor. They thought they might have a better life in America. At the end of the 1800s, there was a lot of **emigration** from Europe. People left Europe to escape from problems there. Many people moved to America.

Immigration, the movement of people to a different country, took place at the end of the 1800s. Because of immigration, millions of people from Europe became Americans. All immigrants had interesting stories about how they left Europe and moved to America. Many older immigrants like to **narrate**, or tell their stories, to their children and grandchildren.

There were also reforms by people who wanted to end slavery. They were part of the antislavery movement. Britain slowly ended slavery in its huge empire. In America, an 1865 law ended slavery forever.

In the next century, in England and America laws were passed that allowed most men to vote. However, women also wanted **suffrage**, or the right to vote. In both countries women worked hard to win suffrage. English women finally won suffrage in 1928. American women won it in 1929.

More New World History Words

emigration

noun leaving one's own country to live in another

immigration

noun people coming into another country to live and work

suffrage

noun the right to vote for a government or leader

Carmen liked to listen to Papi **narrate** how he **immigrated** to America.

Other Useful Words

narrate

verb to tell a story

visualize

verb to create a picture of something in one's mind

Apply the Strategy

Look at a chapter in your textbook that your teacher identifies. Create associations to help you anchor the meaning of any new words you find.

The Right Word

Read each sentence. Look at the word or phrase that is underlined. Write one of the words from the box that means the same thing or almost the same thing as the underlined part of the sentence. Discuss your answers with a partner.

emigrated	labor	progressives	strike	narrate

1. _____ My grandmother likes to <u>tell</u> how she came to America.

2. _____ The union workers wanted higher salaries so they decided to <u>stop working</u>.

3. _____ The <u>people who worked for reform</u> believed young children should not work in factories.

4. _____ We said goodbye to many friends before we <u>moved from our country</u> to America.

5. _____ Progressives wanted to make conditions better for all <u>people who worked hard jobs</u>.

suffrage	visualize	reform	immigration	uprising

6. _____ People who are against something might stage an <u>act of rebellion</u>.

7. _____ Many people wanted to <u>improve</u> society by helping more children go to school.

8. _____ American women won <u>the right to vote</u> in American in 1929.

9. _____ <u>The movement of people to a new country</u> brought millions of people to America.

10. _____ Try to <u>see a picture in your mind of</u> yourself skiing down a tall mountain.

64

Word Challenge: What's Your Reason?

Take turns with a partner reading the statements below out loud. Think of a reason for each statement and write it on the line. Write your reasons in complete sentences. The first one has been done for you.

1. Why might someone **emigrate** from their home country? _They might emigrate to find jobs._

2. Why might someone become a **progressive**? _____

_____

3. Why might workers go on **strike**? _____

_____

4. Why might a group start an **uprising**? _____

_____

Word Challenge: What's Your Answer?

Take turns with a partner reading each question out loud and writing an answer on the line. Answer the questions in complete sentences. The first one has been done for you.

1. What is a reason for **suffrage**? _Everyone should have the right to vote on leaders._

2. What kind of birthday present can you **visualize** for your best friend? _____

_____

3. What kind of **reform** does your school need? _____

_____

4. What kind of **labor** would you not like to do? _____

_____

65

Analogies

Use a word from the box to finish each sentence. Write the word on the line. Discuss your answers with a partner.

labor	progressive	reform	uprising

1 Play is to _____ as order is to confusion.

2 Modern is to _____ as traditional is to conservative.

3 Fight is to _____ as disguise is to cover-up.

4 Improve is to _____ as alter is to change.

Word Study: The Suffix -ive

When you add the suffix -ive to a word, like *progress*, two things happen:

- First, the word changes to an adjective: *progressive*.
- Second, it adds the meaning of "tending to" to the word.

Drop the -e at the end of some words before adding the sufffix -ive.

progress (v.) to move
progressive (adj.) tending to move forward

Fill in the chart. Write the new word created by adding the suffix -ive and its meaning.

	+ -ive	Definition
1 act		
2 create		
3 attract		
4 narrate		

The Language of Testing

How would you answer a question like this on a test?

Which of the following **compares closely to** the meaning of the word *immigration*?

Tip

Compares closely to means *is most like.*

    A. buying a new home
    B. taking a short vacation
    C. leaving one's country
    D. coming into another country to live

Test Strategy: If you see the phrase *compares closely to* on a test, rewrite it using the phrase *is most like.*

1 How could you say the question above in a different way?

_____

_____

Try the strategy again by asking these questions in a different way.

2 Which of the following compares closely to the meaning of the word *uprising*?

    A. uplifting
    B. law
    C. fight
    D. improvement

3 Which of the following compares closely to the meaning of *labor*?

    A. playing tennis
    B. going for a walk
    C. digging a ditch
    D. talking to friends

In Your Vocabulary Journal

Find each of these words in your World History Vocabulary Journal. Working by yourself or with a partner, use the definitions from pages 62 and 63 of your Work Text to complete the rest of the entry for each word.

emigration	immigration	labor	narrate	progressive
reform	strike	suffrage	uprising	visualize

Read the passage below. Think about the meaning of the words in **bold**. Decide if each new word is a *noun*, *verb*, or *adjective*. In the space above each new word, write noun, verb, or adjective. Use this information to help you figure out what the new word means. The first one has been done for you.

 ## The Beginning of World War I

Vocabulary Strategy

Identify if an unfamiliar word is used as a noun, verb, or adjective to help you understand the meaning of the word.

The war that later came to be called World War I began in Europe in 1914. There were four main causes of the war. Nationalism and imperialism were two causes. The third cause was *noun* **militarism**. The nations in Europe built strong, powerful armies.

The fourth cause was that many countries had formed **alliances**. These were agreements that said all nations in the alliance must fight for each other. One alliance was the Central Powers. Germany was its most important nation. The other alliance was called the Allies. England and France were two of the Allies.

At first the United States did not fight for either side. However, Germany became **belligerent** towards the United States. Germany attacked many American ships.

In 1917, the United States declared war against Germany. Americans believed the Allies were fighting to save freedom in Europe. By going to war, Americans **restated** their goal of protecting freedom and democracy.

The United States needed soldiers for the war, so Congress passed a **conscription** law. The law required most young men to serve in the army or navy.

First Call
I Need You in the Navy this Minute!
Our Country will always be proudest of those who answered the FIRST CALL

Navy Recruiting Stations:
34 East 23rd Street New York   115 Flatbush Ave. Brooklyn

New World History Words

alliance
noun   a partnership among a group of countries

belligerent
adjective   showing anger toward someone or something
noun   person, group, or nation that is at war

conscription
noun   a requirement that able citizens join the military

militarism
noun   a desire to have a strong military

Now read this passage and practice the vocabulary strategy again. Identify the part of speech of the new words in **bold**. Write the part of speech near the new word.

The End of World War I

In 1917 Americans quickly **mobilized** their army to fight in World War I. To mobilize an army means to prepare soldiers for war and move them where they will fight. American **civilians**, people who are not in the military, also helped during the war. They grew food for the Allies. They also made weapons.

The American government wanted Americans to believe that it was necessary to fight in World War I. So the government created many **propaganda** posters. Propaganda is information that is used to support a cause. Some propaganda posters encouraged Americans to buy war bonds. These posters **implied**, or suggested, that Americans could not win the war without the help of civilians. Bond money helped pay for the war.

The United States helped the Allies defeat Germany and the other Central Powers. On November 11, 1918, German leaders signed an **armistice**, which was an agreement to stop fighting. The world soon had peace again.

"I've been **mobilized** to help with the war effort!"

More New World History Words

armistice

noun　peace agreement between two fighting countries

civilian

noun　a person who is not in the military

mobilize

verb　to take action, or to get ready for war

propaganda

noun　political information meant to influence people

Other Useful Words

imply

verb　to say something in a way that is not direct

restate

verb　to say or write something again, in a different way

Apply the Strategy

Look at a chapter in your textbook that your teacher identifies. Identify the parts of speech of new words. Use this information to help you figure out the meaning of new words.

Finish the Paragraphs

Use the words in the boxes to finish each paragraph below. Write the correct words in the blanks. One word in each box will not be used. Discuss your answers with a partner.

belligerent	conscription	militarism	armistice	alliances

An important cause of World War I was the building of powerful armies, or

_____, in Europe. Another cause was the growth of agreements
1

between nations called _____. The United States joined the fight
2

when Germany became _____ and attacked American ships.
3

The United States declared war against Germany in 1917. Congress passed a

_____ law that required most young men to serve in the army.
4

propaganda	armistice	depression	civilians	mobilized	implied

In 1917 the United States quickly _____ its army and sent its
5

soldiers to Europe. People who were not in the military were called _____.
6

The government wanted to convince all American civilians to help win the war, so they

made _____ posters. These posters suggested, or
7

_____, that civilians who bought war bonds would help the Allies
8

win. In 1918, Germany lost the war and an _____ agreement said all
9

fighting would stop.

70

Word Challenge: Correct or Incorrect

Read the sentences below either with a partner or by yourself. Write **C** if the sentence is correct, and write **I** if the sentence is incorrect. Rewrite the incorrect sentences.

1 __C__ The two countries ended the war by signing an **armistice**.

2 _____ When Susan joined the navy she became a **civilian**.

_____

3 _____ The government will **mobilize** the troops by sending them into battle.

_____

4 _____ The poster describing the enemy was government **propaganda**.

_____

Word Challenge: Finish the Sentence

Use a word from the box to finish each sentence. Write the correct word on the line. Discuss your choices with a partner.

1 **Conscription** might be unpopular with some people because _they might_

not want to join the military.

2 I would not become friends with a **belligerent** person because _____

_____

3 **Militarism** can be a problem because _____

_____

4 I **restated** what I want for my birthday a few times because _____

_____

Synonyms and Antonyms

Look at each group of words. Circle two words in each group that are synonyms or two words in each group that are antonyms. Then write whether the circled words are synonyms or antonyms on the line below each group. Discuss your answers with a partner.

1 civilian   socialism   **3** belligerent   capitalism

soldier   pharaoh   ally   guild

_____   _____

2 restate   mobilize   **4** imply   suggest

suffrage   repeat   labor   strike

_____   _____

Word Study: The Suffix -ion

When the suffix -ion is added to a verb like *conscript*, it does two things:
- First, it changes its part of speech to a noun: *conscription*.
- Second, it changes its meaning to name an action or the result of an action.

conscript (v.) to require someone to join the military
conscription (n.) a requirement that able citizens join the military

A. Underline the root verb and write a definition for each.

1 dedication _____

2 creation _____

3 invention _____

B. Complete the sentence with one of the words from above.

1 I considered my painting of my dog my best _____ so far.

2 The telephone was an _____ of Alexander Graham Bell.

3 It takes great _____ to become a skilled athlete.

The Language of Testing

How would you answer a question like this on a test?

What is the **main purpose of** propaganda?

A. to tell people the truth about politics
B. to fool the enemy with lies
C. to persuade people to think a certain way
D. to get people to join the army

💡 **Tip**

The word *purpose* can mean *reason* or *use*. The word *main* means that you need to look for the most important purpose.

Test Strategy: If you see a question that uses the word *purpose*, rewrite it using the word *reason* or *use*.

1 How could you say the question above in a different way?

_____

_____

Try the strategy again by asking these questions in a different way.

2 What is the main purpose of an armistice?

   A. to start a war
   B. to stop fighting
   C. to improve battle skills
   D. to enlarge an army

3 For what purpose might a government use conscription?

   A. to enlarge its military
   B. to convince people to vote
   C. to get more money for war
   D. to build better roads

_____   _____

_____   _____

_____   _____

In Your Vocabulary Journal

Find each of these words in your World History Vocabulary Journal. Working by yourself or with a partner, use the definitions from pages 68 and 69 of your Work Text to complete the rest of the entry for each word.

alliance	**armistice**	**belligerent**	**civilian**	**conscription**
imply	**militarism**	**mobilize**	**propaganda**	**restate**

Between the Wars

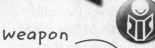

Read the passage below. Think about the meaning of the words in **bold**. Circle familiar root words that are inside of longer new words. Write what you think each word means near it in the passage. The first one has been done for you.

Life Between the Wars

Vocabulary Strategy

Look for words you know to help unlock the meaning of unfamiliar words in the same family. For example: *consume* can help you unlock the meaning of *consumption*.

weapon

The peace treaty that ended World War I was signed in 1919. The treaty required **disarmament** by all countries that had fought in the war. Disarmament means a nation makes and owns less weapons. The treaty also forced Germany to pay **reparations**, or money for war damages, to the Allies.

Some nations felt that the punishment was unfair. Germany's economy began to suffer. During the 1930s, the economies of other countries weakened, too. Now the Allies needed all the money they could make from trade.

After the war, Britain and France were given mandates, or territories they had to control. Britain and France had to prepare these colonies to rule themselves. Several countries in the Middle East such as Iraq and Syria became mandates.

The 1920s brought wealth and **prosperity** to the United States. Americans bought cars, radios, and clothing. People hoped that these good years would last forever. Today, we can **evaluate** history and clearly see the causes of the worldwide depression and war to come. In the 1920s, though, only a very few people could see these coming problems.

New World History Words

disarmament

noun   the act of decreasing the number of weapons a country has

prosperity

noun   wealth or success

reparations

noun   money paid by losing country to cover damages after a war

Now read the passage below and practice the vocabulary strategy again. Circle any familiar words inside of larger new words that might help you figure out what these words mean.

 # Hard Times

Many social problems in the United States have been blamed on the **Prohibition** era. Prohibition lasted from 1919 to 1933 when the sale of alcoholic beverages was against the law.

This was also the time of economic depressions around the world. In 1929, the Great Depression began. The Great Depression could be **distinguished**, or set apart, from other depressions because it was much more severe. One cause of this depression was the lack of **consumption** of products. People were not buying and using many things, so prices dropped. Many farms and factories went out of business. Millions of people lost their jobs and homes.

At least in part, depressions allowed the ideas of **fascism** to spread in Italy and Germany. Under fascism, a country is ruled by a dictator who has total power. In Germany, the fascists were called Nazis. Their cruel dictator was Adolf Hitler.

Fascists also believed in **totalitarianism**. This means the government has total power over the people. Russia and Japan had totalitarian governments.

 ## More New World History Words

consumption
> *noun*   buying products and using resources

fascism
> *noun*   a system in which a strong military leader runs the government

prohibition
> *noun*   the act of making something popular illegal, or the period of time when alcoholic beverages were illegal in the U.S.

totalitarianism
> *noun*   a system in which one political party controls everything

 ## Other Useful Words

distinguish
> *verb*   to see or understand the difference between things

evaluate
> *verb*   to judge the quality of something, or to place a value on it

Consumption is hard when there is no **prosperity**!

Apply the Strategy

Look at a chapter in your textbook that your teacher identifies. Use familiar root words to help you figure out the meaning of new words.

Find the Word

Write a word from the box next to each clue. Then read the word that is formed with the boxed letters. The word answers the question below.

| prohibition | fascist | prosperity | fascism | disarmament |
| totalitarian | reparations | evaluated | distinguish | consumption |

1 to make something illegal __ __ [ ] __ __ __ __ __ __ __ __

2 a removal of weapons __ __ __ __ __ __ __ __ __ [ ] __ __ __

3 buying and using products __ __ __ __ __ __ [ ] __ __ __ __

4 ruled by a dictator __ __ __ [ ] __ __ __ __ __ __

5 money for war damages [ ] __ __ __ __ __ __ __ __ __ __

6 judged __ __ [ ] __ __ __ __ __ __

7 a government with total control __ __ [ ] __ __ __ __ __ __ __ __ __

8 belief held by the Nazis __ __ __ __ __ [ ] __ __

9 a time of wealth __ __ [ ] __ __ __ __ __ __ __

10 to tell apart __ __ __ __ [ ] __ __ __ __ __ __

What was the money that Germany paid the Allies called?

__ __ __ __ __ __ __ __ __ __ __ s

Word Challenge: Quick Pick

Read the following questions aloud with a partner. Write an answer for each on the lines below. Write your answers in complete sentences. The first one has been done for you.

1 What was outlawed during **prohibition**: guns or alcohol? _Alcohol was outlawed_

during prohibition.

2 Would a capitalist government encourage sanctions or **consumption**? _____

_____

3 Is **fascism** a belief in a powerful state or a powerful population? _____

_____

4 What would a country be doing during **disarmament**: increasing its military or decreasing

its weaponry? _____

Word Challenge: Which Word?

Take turns reading the sentences below out loud with a partner. Together, think of a statement for each that gives a clue about its meaning. Write your statement next to the word. The first one has been done for you.

1 totalitarianism ___"I control people's lives."_____

2 prosperity _____

3 reparations _____

4 evaluate _____

5 prohibition _____

Analogies

Use a word from the box to finish each sentence. Write the word on the line. Discuss your answers with a partner.

| totalitarianism | prosperity | disarmament | fascism | consumption |

1 Democracy is to president as _____ is to dictator.

2 Depression is to hard times as _____ is to good times.

3 Conserve is to save as _____ is to buy and use.

4 Liberty is to democracy as government control is to _____.

5 Arms are to war time as _____ is to peace time.

Word Study: The Prefix *dis-*

When the prefix *dis-* is added to a word, it changes the meaning of the word. The prefix *dis-* has several meanings, but the basic meaning is *opposite*.

arm (v.) to supply with weapons
disarm (n.) to reduce the number of or to do away with weapons

Add the prefix *dis-* to the words below and write a definition for each. Use a dictionary to check your spelling and definitions.

		+ *dis-*	Definition
1	believe		
2	connect		
3	place		
4	respect		

The Language of Testing

How would you answer a question like this on a test?

What is a **characteristic** of consumption?

    A. People start savings accounts.
    B. People mend old clothes and socks.
    C. People buy many pairs of new shoes.
    D. People take the bus instead of driving.

 Tip

A *characteristic* of a thing is something that it usually has or does.

Test Strategy: If you see question that uses the word *characteristic*, rewrite it to ask for the thing that is true about the subject of the sentence.

1 How could you say the question above in a different way?

_____

_____

Try the strategy again by asking these questions in a different way.

2 What is a characteristic of totalitarianism?

    A. one powerful political party
    B. many political parties with little power
    C. two political parties with equal power
    D. two main political parties and several lesser parties

3 What is a characteristic of fascism?

    A. pride in one's country
    B. good state benefits
    C. a powerful voting public
    D. strong government control

_____

_____

_____

In Your Vocabulary Journal

Find each of these words in your World History Vocabulary Journal. Working by yourself or with a partner, use the definitions from pages 74 and 75 of your Work Text to complete the rest of the entry for each word.

consumption	disarmament	distinguish	evaluate	fascism
prohibition	prosperity	reparation	totalitarianism	

World War II

Read the passage below. Think about the meanings of the new words in **bold**. Underline any definitions that might help you figure out what the new words mean. The first one has been done for you.

The Early Years of World War II

Vocabulary Strategy

Look for definitions in the text to help you figure out the meanings of new words.

World War II began in 1939. Germany's dictator, Adolf Hitler, ordered the **invasion**, or <u>attack</u>, of Poland. Then Britain and France went to war against Germany. Hitler quickly conquered Poland, France, and many countries in Europe. Only Britain remained free to fight Hitler. During this time, Japan conquered countries in Asia.

In 1939 the United States wanted **neutrality**. This means it would not fight for either side. But on December 7, 1941, Japan attacked Pearl Harbor. This American naval base was in Hawaii. Thousands of Americans were killed. The United States quickly went to war against Japan, Germany, and Italy.

American leaders **assessed**, or carefully guessed, the number of soldiers and weapons they needed for the war. The leaders also knew there was not enough food to feed both Americans at home and soldiers in Europe and Asia. Therefore, Americans received **rations**, or limited amounts of certain foods, such as sugar and meat. Non-food items, like things made of silk and rubber, were also rationed.

Americans planned to win **liberation**, or freedom, for the conquered countries in Europe and Asia.

New World History Words

invasion

noun   an attack on a country

liberation

noun   freedom from the control of another country or group

neutrality

noun   refusing to choose a side or express a preference

ration

noun   a limited amount of something

verb   to limit the amount of something

Now read the passage below and practice the vocabulary strategy again. Underline any definitions in the text that might help you figure out what the words in **bold** mean.

The End of World War II

From 1941 to 1945, Americans fought with the Allies against Germany and Italy. They fought against Japan in Asia. The Allies helped many countries become free, including France.

Adolf Hitler planned the **genocide** of Europe's Jewish people. Genocide is the killing of an entire group of people. Hitler spread hatred and lies against the Jews throughout Europe. In addition, he had huge death camps built. By the end of World War II, six million Jews had been killed in the death camps.

Communists, socialists, and Roma, or Gypsies, were also killed in these camps. The killing of six million Jews and members of other groups during World War II is called the **Holocaust**.

World War II ended in 1945. Then the Allies began the **occupation** of Germany. Occupation means the control of a defeated nation by the winning nation. American soldiers also occupied Japan. The **demilitarization** of Japan took place, too. Japan could not have an army or own war weapons.

More New World History Words

blockade
noun   a barrier that prevents supplies from getting into a country

demilitarization
noun   the act of removing military forces from an area

genocide
noun   the planned murder of an entire race

Holocaust
noun   the planned murder of over 6 million Jews and members of other certain groups in Europe during WWII

occupation
noun   the act of capturing a country by force, or a job or profession

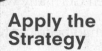

Other Useful Words

assess
verb   to figure out the amount of something, or to figure out the truth of a situation

plagiarize
verb   to claim someone else's ideas or work as your own

Apply the Strategy

Look at a chapter in your textbook that your teacher identifies. Use definitions in the text to help you figure out the meanings of new words you find.

Finish the Sentences

Use a word from the box to finish each sentence. Write the correct word on the line. Discuss your choices with a partner.

invasion	assess	rations	genocide	neutrality

1. World War II began with the German attack, or _____, of Poland.

2. In 1939 the United States did not fight for either side because its policy was _____.

3. The mass murder of an entire people is _____.

4. Limited amounts of food that people were allowed to buy during the war were called _____.

5. The United States had to guess, or _____, how many soldiers it would need to fight in World War II.

liberation	Holocaust	occupation	demilitarization	plagiarize

6. If you _____ a story, you are copying it instead of creating it yourself.

7. The killing of six million Jews during World War II was the _____.

8. When Germany was defeated, _____ and freedom came to countries that had been captured.

9. The United States and three other countries controlled Germany after the war during a period called the _____ of that country.

10. After the war, Japan could not have an army due to a policy of _____.

Word Challenge: Word Association

Take turns with a partner reading the groups of words below. Write the word from the lesson that best goes with each group. The first one has been done for you.

1 _____blockade_____ barrier, wall

2 _____ not taking sides, no preference

3 _____ release, freedom

4 _____ job, profession, taking control of a country

5 _____ steal ideas, copy, cheat

Word Challenge: What's Your Reason?

Take turns with a partner reading each question below out loud and writing an answer on the line. Answer the questions in complete sentences. The first one has been done for you.

1 Why do librarians need to **assess** the books in the library? _Librarians need to_ _know whether there are enough books in good shape._

2 Why would a nation **occupy** an enemy country after a war? _____

_____

3 Why a might a nation maintain **neutrality** during a war? _____

_____

4 Why should students learn about the **Holocaust**? _____

_____

5 Why are there **rations** for food during a war? _____

_____

Synonyms and Antonyms

Look at each group of words. Circle two words in each group that are synonyms or two words in each group that are antonyms. Then write whether the circled words are synonyms or antonyms on the line below each group.

1 invasion   attack

archaeology   feudalism

_____

3 occupation   plagiarize

neutrality   copy

_____

2 liberation   reform

capture   corporation

_____

4 ration   peasant

empire   allowance

_____

Word Study: The Suffix -ation

When the suffix -ation is added to a verb such as occupy, it does two things:

- First, it changes the verb to a noun: occupation.
- Second, it changes the word's meaning. The word now names the process or result of something.

Drop the -e from the end of a word before adding -ation.

occupy (v.) to take control of something by force
occupation (n.) the act of capturing a country by force

Add the suffix -ation to each root verb to make a new word. Write a definition for each one. Use a dictionary to check your spelling and definitions.

	+ -ation	Definition
1 confirm		
2 adapt		
3 reserve		
4 reform		

The Language of Testing

How would you answer a question like this on a test?

Each of the following statements is true

except

- A. Genocide is racially based murder.
- B. An invasion is an attack on a country.
- C. Neutrality is capturing a country by force.
- D. An occupation is a profession.

Tip

The word *except* means you should look for something that means the opposite of the word or phrase before *except*. The opposite of true is false. So in this question, you should look for the answer that is false.

Test Strategy: Make sure you understand the question. Read it carefully. Then, if it has the word *except* in it, ask the question in a different way. Remember that you are looking for the statement that is false.

1 How could you say the question above in a different way?

_____

_____

Try the strategy again by asking these questions in a different way.

2 All of these are acts of war except

- A. invasion
- B. occupation
- C. genocide
- D. ration

3 All of these signs might be seen at a blockade except

- A. Do not enter.
- B. No departure.
- C. Stop!
- D. Welcome.

_____   _____

_____   _____

_____   _____

In Your Vocabulary Journal

Find each of these words in your World History Vocabulary Journal. Working by yourself or with a partner, use the definitions from pages 80 and 81 of your Work Text to complete the rest of the entry for each word.

assess   blockade   demilitarization   genocide   Holocaust   invasion

liberation   neutrality   occupation   plagiarize   ration

Read the passage below. Think about the meanings of the new words in **bold**. Underline any examples or descriptions you find that might help you figure out what these words mean. The first one has been done for you.

The Cold War Years

Vocabulary Strategy

Use examples and descriptions in the text to help you figure out the meaning of new words. Look for clues like *such as*, *for example*, or *like*. Look for pictures that might show you what a new word means, too.

The years between 1945 and 1991 were called the Cold War. During those years, the Soviet Union, now called Russia, was a communist country. During the Cold War, the United States followed a policy called **containment**. <u>It tried to prevent countries from having communist governments.</u> The United States helped rebuild Japan so it would not become a communist country.

After 1945, Americans feared that **nuclear** weapons, weapons with atomic bombs, might be used during a war. The United States and the Soviet Union signed treaties to limit the number of weapons each nation could have.

Britain and other nations in Europe became **welfare** states after 1945. In a welfare state, the government pays for many services that people need. In Britain the government provided everyone with medical care and pensions. However, the government had to **clarify**, or make clear, which services it would provide.

After World War I, many nations experienced **urbanization**. Millions of people moved from towns and farms to cities.

New World History Words

containment

noun the act of keeping something, such as another country's power, within limits

nuclear

adjective having to do with weapons that explode by using energy released from splitting atoms

urbanization

noun a process in which city populations grow and rural areas shrink

welfare

noun person's health or comfort, or money paid by government to unemployed, poor, or sick people

Now read this passage and practice the vocabulary strategy again. Underline any examples and descriptions in the passage. Draw an arrow from each to the word it describes.

 ## After the Cold War

When communism ended in the Soviet Union in 1989, many people thought this would bring world peace. Instead, countries used economic **sanctions**, such as boycotts, to punish enemies. When sanctions make goods hard to get, people suffer from the **inflation** of prices on the things they need.

Not every country or group is powerful enough to fight a war or apply sanctions. These groups rely on **terrorism** to **protest** things they want to change. Like inflation, terrorism hurts civilians. However, it is much more dangerous. Nobody knows when or where terrorists will attack.

Some terrorists actions are very large and well planned. On September 11, 2001, terrorists crashed airplanes into the World Trade Center towers and the Pentagon. Passengers on another plane fought the terrorists, causing their plane to crash in a Pennsylvania field. Nearly 3,000 people died in these attacks. The **international** community supported the U.S. with donations of money and goods. For example, one very poor Masai tribe in Africa presented a gift of 14 cows to the U.S.

 ### More New World History Words

inflation
  noun   an increase in price of goods
international
  adjective   involving different countries
protest
  verb   to take action against something
  noun   an action taken against something
sanctions
  noun   actions taken against a country that has broken international laws
terrorism
  noun   acts of violence against civilians

 ### Other Useful Words

clarify
  verb   to make something easier to understand
synthesize
  verb   to combine information from many sources

Chris found a good use for **inflation**.

 ## Apply the Strategy

Look at a chapter in your textbook that your teacher identifies. Use explanations, descriptions, and pictures to help you figure out the meaning of any new words you find.

Matching

Finish the sentences in Group A with words from Group B. Write the letter of the word on the line. Discuss your choices with a partner.

Group A

1. The American policy to stop the spread of communism was called _____.

2. Dangerous weapons that contain atomic bombs are _____ weapons.

3. When you try to make facts clear and easy to understand, you _____ the facts.

4. When many people move to cities and the cities grow larger, there is _____.

5. When a government provides services like health care, the country becomes a _____ state.

Group B

A. nuclear
B. urbanization
C. welfare
D. containment
E. clarify

Group A

6. _____ means something that happens between two or more nations.

7. An increase in the price of goods is _____.

8. When you combine different facts into one report, you _____ information.

9. We went to _____ the building of a new mall on the swamp.

10. The use of violence against civilians is called _____.

Group B

F. synthesize
G. international
H. terrorism
I. protest
J. inflation

Word Challenge: Correct or Incorrect

Read the sentences below either with a partner or by yourself. Write **C** if the sentence is correct, and write **I** if the sentence is incorrect. Rewrite the incorrect sentences.

1 __C__ Because of **inflation,** we had to cut back on our spending.

2 _____ You need a passport for **international** travel.

_____

3 _____ We **protested** the new bookstore by buying all our books there.

_____

4 _____ **Urbanization** takes place in large urban areas.

_____

Word Challenge: Quick Pick

Read each question with a partner or by yourself. Decide on the best answer. Explain your answer. The first one has been done for you.

1 Does **urbanization** mean the growth of farms or the growth of cities? _Urbanization_

means that people move away from farming areas to the cities and cities grow larger.

2 Who might receive **welfare**: a wealthy doctor or a poor father of five? _____

_____

3 Does **inflation** mean that food will be cheaper or more expensive? _____

_____

4 Does **containment** help or prevent a country from having too much power?

_____

Analogies

Use a word from the box to finish each sentence. Discuss your answers with a partner.

| clarify | synthesize | international | inflation | urbanization |

1 National is about one country as _____ is about many countries.

2 Divide is to separate as combine is to _____.

3 Confuse is to mix up as explain is to _____.

4 Loss of jobs is to depression as high prices are to _____.

5 Rural is to country as _____ is to cities.

Word Study: The Suffixes -or and -er

When you add the suffix -or or -er to a verb like protest, you do two things:

- First, you change the word from a verb to a noun: protestor.
- Second, you change the meaning of the word. The new word names a person or thing that does a job.

protest (v.) to show openly you are against something
protestor (n.) someone who shows openly that he or she is against something

Circle the -er and the -or words.

The elevator was broken, so Susan was forced to walk up the stairs. When she reached the

fourth floor, Susan presented her idea to the patent lawyer. Her invention was a new computer

program for illustrators. To help sell her invention, Susan next had a meeting on the fifth floor

with a marketing manager. The two of them made a plan for selling her program. She worked

with an advertiser and a famous painter to create an advertisement.

She had an actor in mind to present her idea to the public. She hoped he would be available.

The Language of Testing

How would you answer a question like this on a test?

Identify something people would be most likely to protest.

    A. a new clothing store
    B. a high school graduation
    C. a controversial movie
    D. the birth of a baby

 Tip

When you *identify*, you point out or name something. In a test question, *identify* means to *choose* or *pick* the correct answer.

Test Strategy: Make sure you understand the question. Read it carefully. If you see a question that uses the word *identify*, rewrite it using the words *choose* or *pick*.

1 How would you say the question above in a different way?

_____

_____

Try the strategy again by rewriting the questions using the words *choose* or *pick*.

2 Identify the correct definition for the word *inflation*.

    A. an increase in the number of citizens
    B. an increase in the cost of goods
    C. an increase in the number of troops
    D. an increase in the amount of food

_____

_____

_____

3 Identify someone who would probably *not* receive welfare.

    A. an unemployed person
    B. a poor person
    C. a student on a scholarship
    D. a sick person

_____

_____

_____

In Your Vocabulary Journal

Find each of these words in your World History Vocabulary Journal. Working by yourself or with a partner, use the definitions from pages 86 and 87 of your Work Text to complete the rest of the entry for each word.

clarify	containment	inflation	international	nuclear	protest
sanctions	synthesize	terrorism	urbanization	welfare	

Glossary

Aa

absolutism (abs uh **loo** tiz **uhm**)
noun   a system in which one ruler has total power over a country (*A country that practices **absolutism** is despotic.*)

alliance (uh **ly** uhns)
noun   a partnership among a group of countries (*It is important for countries to form **alliances** so that they will have support in the event of a war.*)

ancient (**ayn** chuhnt)
adjective   belonging to the distant past (*The scientist was studying **ancient** bones that were almost 400 years old.*)

apprentice (uh **prehn** tis)
noun   a young person who works for no pay to learn a skill (*After being an **apprentice** for two years, Marcos felt he was ready to work alone.*)

archaeology (**ahr** kee **ahl** uh jee)
noun   the study of the buildings, tools, and way of life of people of the past (*Alim wanted to study **archaeology** because of his love for ancient cities.*)

aristocracy (ar ih **stah** kruh **see**)
noun   a class of people who have high position in society (*Kings and Queens are members of the **aristocracy**.*)

armistice (**ahr** muh stis)
noun   peace agreement between two fighting countries (*The two countries were tired of battling, so they signed an **armistice**.*)

articulate (ahr **tik** yoo **layt**)
verb   to express thoughts clearly and easily (*He was not able to **articulate** what he really meant.*)

artifact (**ahrt** uh **fakt**)
noun   a tool or object that is made by and used by a person (*The Neanderthals used stone weapons that archaeologists call **artifacts**.*)

assess (uh **sehs**)
verb   to figure out the amount of something, or to figure out the truth of a situation (*After the hurricane, the city officials came back to **assess** the damages.*)

assimilation (uh **sim** uh **lay** shuhn)
noun   the act of learning or adopting the ideas, customs and lifestyle of another culture (***Assimilation** was difficult for Andre because he had never lived in a tropical country.*)

autocracy (aw **tah** kruh see)
noun   a government controlled by one person who has total power (*The citizens do not have their own rights in an **autocracy**.*)

Bb

barter (**bahrt** uhr)
verb   to trade goods for other goods (*They were forced to **barter** when they ran out of food.*)

belligerent (buh **lij** uhr uhnt)
adjective   showing anger toward someone or something (*As the crowd disagreed with him, the speaker became more **belligerent**.*)

noun   person, group, or nation that is at war (*The **belligerents** were at war for almost two years.*)

blockade (blah **kayd**)
noun   a barrier that prevent supplies from getting into a country (*The soldiers formed a **blockade** to keep the enemy from escaping.*)

bureaucracy (byoo **rah** kruh see)
noun   all of the rules followed by a government department, or a system in which many people in many jobs help run the government (*In a **bureaucracy**, there are many different political leaders who must follow strict rules.*)

Cc

capitalism (**kap** uht uhl **iz** uhm)
  noun   system in which property, business, and industry are privately owned (*The business owner was thankful to be living in a country that practiced **capitalism**.*)

characterize (**kar** uhk tuhr **yz**)
  verb   to describe someone or something by a specific thing (*Adolf Hitler was **characterized** by his tyrannical behavior.*)

chivalry (**shiv** uhl ree)
  noun   the rules that knights were required to follow (*Honor was important to the code of **chivalry**.*)

civilian (suh **vil** yuhn)
  noun   a person who is not in the military (*Lan was in the military for ten years, and then he became a **civilian**.*)

clarify (**klar** uh fy)
  verb   to make something easier to understand (*The manager **clarified** the rules of the office for the new employees.*)

colony (**kahl** uh nee)
  noun   a settlement or land that belongs to another country (*The **colony** was inside their border, but it belonged to another country.*)

commercial (kuh **mur** shuhl)
  noun   done for a profit (*The businessmen wanted to make a lot of money, so they read books on **commercial** business.*)

commodity (kuh **mahd** uh tee)
  noun   something that is sold or traded (*When Emilia learned to make bags, she turned them into a **commodity**.*)

communism (**kahm** yoo **niz** uhm)
  noun   a system in which the government controls all businesses and decides what factories and farmers will produce (*In **communism**, the government owns your home and your business.*)

compass (**kuhm** puhs)
  noun   a tool that is used for finding directions (*The campers used a **compass** to find their way back to the tent.*)

compile (kuhm **pyl**)
  verb   to put together (*James **compiled** a list of resources to write his article.*)

conquest (**kangk** kwehst)
  noun   the act of taking over a country or group of people (*During the **conquest**, the victims tried to hide from the invaders.*)

conservative (kuhn **sur** vuh tiv)
  noun   someone who resists change (*My dad says that he is a **conservative** when it comes to economics.*)

  adjective   resisting change (*The **conservative** group voted to leave all the rules the same.*)

conscription (kuhn **skript** shuhn)
  noun   a requirement that able citizens join the military (*After the **conscription** took place, the military had 100 new soldiers.*)

consumption (kuhn **suhmp** chuhn)
  noun   buying products and using resources (*One effect of **consumption** is a growing number of advertisements.*)

containment (kuhn **tayn** muhnt)
  noun   the act of keeping something, such as another country's power, within limits (*After the collapse of the Soviet Union, Russia's **containment** of Eastern European countries ended.*)

contradict (**kahn** truh **dikt**)
  verb   to go against or say the opposite of something (*The business owners **contradicted** the socialist ideas.*)

corporation (**kawr** puh **ray** shuhn)
  noun   a large business or company (*Most **corporations** have a main office that controls everything.*)

counterrevolutionary
(**kownt** uhr **rehv** uh **lu** shuh **nehr** ee)
  adjective   about policies or people who want to reverse the effects of social or political change (*The revolutionists faced an upcoming confrontation from the **counterrevolutionaries**.*)

critique (kri **teek**)
  noun   to criticize or judge (*Maria **critiqued** the three students applying for a job.*)

crusade (kroo **sayd**)

noun a long effort to achieve something for a cause (*Felipa began a **crusade** to end violence in her country.*)

verb to fight hard to achieve something for a cause (*The civil rights activists **crusaded** for an end to discrimination.*)

cultivate (**kul** tuh **vayt**)

verb to prepare land to grow crops, or to develop something to make it better (*The farmers **cultivated** the land just in time for the rainy season.*)

culture (**kuhl** chuhr)

noun the shared traditions and beliefs of a group of people (*Gloria asked her mother to teach her about the Spanish **culture**.*)

Dd

decline (dee **klyn**)

verb to become less in amount or importance (*Hao **declined** the job that his boss offered him.*)

noun a process by which something becomes less in amount or importance (*During an economic hardship, chocolate sales take a serious **decline**.*)

demilitarization (dee **mil** uh tuh ry **zay** shuhn)

noun the act of removing military forces from an area (*The **demilitarization** followed the peace agreement.*)

democracy (di **mahk** ruh see)

noun a system of government in which people choose their own laws and leaders (*In a **democracy**, the people feel they have a voice in important issues.*)

depression (dee **prehsh** uhn)

noun a time of little economic activity, or a period of unemployment and poverty (*During the **depression**, Miguel knew he could not ask his parents to buy him anything.*)

despotism (**des** puh **tiz** uhm)

noun cruel and unfair government by very powerful rulers (***Despotism** requires a country's people to be completely obedient.*)

dictator (**dik tayt** uhr)

noun a leader who has total control in a country (*The people disliked their **dictator**, but they were too afraid to rebel against him.*)

differentiate (**dif** uhr **ehn** shee **ayt**)

verb to show the difference between things (*Mr. Graham asked his students to **differentiate** between treason and nationalism.*)

diplomacy (duh **ploh** muh see)

noun the process of developing good relationships between countries (*Because of its **diplomacy** policies, the country has many allies.*)

disarmament (dis **ahr** muh muhnt)

noun the act of decreasing the number of weapons a country has (*The United States had agreed to **disarmament** so it made less weapons after World War I.*)

distinguish (di **sting** gwish)

verb to see or understand the difference between things (*It was difficult for Jill to **distinguish** between the two rocks.*)

domesticate (**doh** mehs ti **kayt**)

verb to tame animals and grow plants for human use (*Tam was covered in scratches after trying to **domesticate** the wild cat.*)

dynasty (**dy** nuh stee)

noun a ruling family (*The Chou **dynasty** of China was forced to abandon its capital to avoid barbarian invasion.*)

Ee

emigration (**ehm** ih **gray** shuhn)

noun leaving one's own country to live in another (***Emigration** was Selma's only option because she could not find work in her own country.*)

empire (**ehm** pyr)

noun a number of countries that are all under the control of one ruling country (*Peru, Ecuador, and Chile were all part of an **empire**.*)

enlightenment (ehn **lyt** in muhnt)

noun   the act of giving or gaining knowledge about something, or the movement in the 18th century based on science and reason *(She experienced **enlightenment** when the missionary told his story.)*

ethics (**ehth** iks)

noun   beliefs and rules about what is right and wrong *(Her **ethics** are based on what her parents have taught her.)*

evaluate (ee **val** yoo **ayt**)

verb   to judge the quality of something, or to place a value on it *(Pablo **evaluated** the silk that he gained from his exchange of tools.)*

expansion (ehk **span** shuhn)

noun   the act of becoming greater in size or amount *(When the company gained a large customer base, they decided it was time for **expansion**.)*

Ff

fallacy (**fal** uh see)

noun   A false or mistaken idea *(When Joan asked Bill about the Loch Ness monster, he told her it was a **fallacy**.)*

fascism (**fash** iz uhm)

noun   a system in which a strong military leader runs the government *(Americans control their own lives because their government does not believe in **fascism**.)*

feudalism (**fyood** uhl iz uhm)

noun   a system in which people were given land to work on and were protected by people with more power *(**Feudalism** protected the peasants from barbarian raids.)*

formulate (**fawr** myoo **layt**)

verb   to plan or develop something *(The farmers **formulated** a plan to grow twice as much corn as last year.)*

Gg

generalize (**jen** uhr uhl **yz**)

verb   to say that something is almost always true, or to leave out the details *(Sometimes leaders **generalize** about people in other countries.)*

genocide (**jehn** uh **syd**)

noun   the planned murder of an entire race *(**Genocide** took place before and during World War II when Adolf Hitler ordered the death of six million Jews.)*

guild (**gild**)

noun   an organization of people who do the same job or work at the same skill *(In medieval times, men would form **guilds** to protect one another.)*

Hh

heretic (**hehr** eh tik)

noun   someone whose beliefs and actions go against accepted beliefs *(In the past, some scientists were called **heretics**.)*

hierarchy (**hy** uhr **ahr** kee)

noun   a way of organizing people into different levels of importance *(In the royal **hierarchy**, the King and Queen are at the top.)*

Holocaust (**haw** loh **kawst**)

noun   the planned murder of over six million Jews and members of other certain groups in Europe during World War II *(The **Holocaust** is one of the most devastating acts of genocide in our world's history.)*

Ii

immigration (**im** uh **gray** shuhn)

noun   people coming into another country to live and work *(When **immigration** became heavy, some countries put more guards around their borders.)*

imperialism (**im pihr** ee uhl **iz** uhm)

noun   a system in which a rich and powerful country has control over other countries *(**Imperialism** by the West caused Africa and Asia to try and drive the foreigners away.)*

imply (im **ply**)

    verb   to say something in a way that is not direct (*Sue's insult to the teacher was **implied**, but the teacher understood what she meant.*)

industrialization
(in **duhs** tree uhl ih **zay** shuhn)

    noun   the development of many factories (*When **industrialization** takes place, many new job opportunities become available.*)

infer (in **fur**)

    verb   to come to a conclusion (*Based on her accent, he **inferred** that the woman was from another country.*)

inflation (in **flay** shuhn)

    noun   an increase in the price of goods (*Sonia's luxurious lifestyle became limited because of **inflation**.*)

international (in tuhr **nash** uh nuhl)

    adjective   involving different countries (*The **international** spy spoke seven different languages.*)

invasion (in **vay** zhuhn)

    noun   an attack on a country (*The President prepared his military for a possible **invasion**.*)

isolationism (**eye** suh **lay** shuhn iz **uhm**)

    noun   a policy of avoiding contact with other countries (*Some countries believe in **isolationism** because they do not want to be involved in war.*)

Ll

labor (**lay** buhr)

    noun   work, or the people working in a factory (*The **labor** union went on strike to try and get more money.*)

liberation (**lib** uhr **ay** shuhn)

    noun   freedom from the control of another country or group (***Liberation** took place in Europe after the Cold War.*)

Mm

manor (man **uhr**)

    noun   a large country house on a large area of land with several smaller buildings around it (*The **manor** had been passed down through generations.*)

mechanization (**mehk** uh ni **zay** shuhn)

    noun   process of using machines to do more tasks (***Mechanization** allowed people to instantly produce more goods than ever before.*)

medieval (mi **dee** vuhl)

    adjective   describing something belonging to the period of time between AD 476 and AD 1500 (*Yuri studied **medieval** literature because of his interest in the Middle Ages.*)

mercantilism (**mur** kuhn til **iz** uhm)

    noun   a policy of building wealth through trade (***Mercantilism** allows people to own a variety of goods.*)

migration (my **gray** shuhn)

    noun   movement from one region or country to another (*Ana looked up just in time to see a large **migration** of birds.*)

militarism (**mil** uh tuh **riz** uhm)

    noun   a desire to have a strong military (***Militarism** is important to all leaders who are concerned with protecting their country.*)

missionary (**mish** uhn **ehr** ee)

    noun   a person sent to a foreign place to teach about his or her religion (*The students gathered around the **missionary** for their religious lesson.*)

mobilize (**moh** buh **lyz**)

    verb   to take action, or to get ready for war (*The troops **mobilized** when they heard gunfire.*)

moderate (**mahd** uhr it)

adjective   avoiding extreme behavior or beliefs (The **moderate** political group did not participate in the protests.)

noun   someone who avoids extreme behavior or beliefs (The **moderate** had the same hairstyle for twenty years.)

monarchy (**mahn** ahr kee)

noun   a country that is ruled by a king or queen (Royalists support countries that believe in **monarchy**.)

monopoly (muh **nahp** uh lee)

noun   complete control of products or services by a company, person, or state (The telephone company had a **monopoly** on long distance service.)

monotheism (**mahn** oh **thee** iz uhm)

noun   a belief in one God (Christians believe strongly in **monotheism**.)

Nn

narrate (**nar** ayt)

verb   to tell a story (Native Americans have a tradition of **narrating** their history.)

nationalism (**nash** uh nuhl **iz** uhm)

noun   strong feelings of loyalty to one's country (Our feelings of **nationalism** became stronger after we came home from our trip out of the country.)

navigation (**nav** uh **gay** shuhn)

noun   the process of planning a course for travel (Being a ship captain equipped Diego with great **navigation** skills.)

neutrality (noo **tral** uh tee)

noun   refusing to choose a side or express a preference (Switzerland is well known for its **neutrality**.)

nobility (noh **bil** uh tee)

noun   a group of people in society who have a high rank (Natalya dreamed of being a part of the **nobility** every time she saw the princess on T.V.)

nomad (**no** mad)

noun   a person who moves from place to place to find food (Ivan was glad that his parents were **nomads**, because he got to travel all over the world.)

nuclear (**noo** klee uhr)

adjective   having to do with weapons that explode by using energy released from splitting atoms (**Nuclear** weapons contain very powerful bombs.)

Oo

occupation (**ahk** yoo **pay** shuhn)

noun   the act of capturing a country by force, or a job or profession (The **occupation** of the small island was helpful because they needed to build a naval base in the Atlantic Ocean.)

Pp

paraphrase (**par** uh **frayz**)

verb   to reword something spoken or written (He **paraphrased** his speech for the group that came in late.)

parliament (**pahr** luh muhnt)

noun   a group of people in some countries who make the laws (The **parliament** discussed the future of Great Britain.)

peasant (**pez** uhnt)

noun   a person of lower rank that works on the land (The two **peasants** stood on a hill, watching the flock of sheep.)

perspective (puhr **spehk** tiv)

noun   a specific way of thinking about something (From the peasant's **perspective**, the prices on produce were very high.)

pharaoh (**fehr** oh)

noun   a king in ancient Egypt (The monuments of the **pharaohs** are artifacts that are studied in great detail.)

philosophy (fi **lahs** uh fee)

noun   the study of ideas (Cho's **philosophy** about animal protection caused her to become a vegetarian.)

plagiarize (**play** juh **ryz**)
verb to claim someone else's ideas or work as your own (*Sara was expelled for* **plagiarizing** *a poem.*)

plague (**playg**)
noun a deadly disease that spreads very quickly (*A* **plague** *can wipe out an entire country.*)

polytheism (**pahl** ih **thee** iz uhm)
noun belief in more than one god (*Hindus worship many gods, so we say that Hindus practice* **polytheism**.)

predict (pree **dikt**)
verb to say what will happen in the future (*The reporter asked the president to* **predict** *when the war would be over.*)

prehistoric (**pree** his **tawr** ik)
noun people and things that existed before history was written down (*Dinosaurs are considered* **prehistoric**.)

progressive (proh **grehs** iv)
noun someone who wants to improve society (*Lee considered himself a* **progressive** *because he was interested in improving his community.*)

prohibition (**proh** uh **bish** uhn)
noun the act of making something illegal, or the period of time when alcoholic beverages were illegal in the U.S. (*During* **prohibition**, *many people began making their own alcohol.*)

propaganda (**prahp** uh **gan** duh)
noun political information meant to influence people (*The activists got together to paint some anti-war* **propaganda** *posters.*)

prosperity (prahs **pehr** uh tee)
noun wealth or success (*At the end of his speech, he wished happiness and* **prosperity** *to us all.*)

protest (**proh** tehst)
noun an action taken against something (*We planned a* **protest** *against the proposed amendment to the Constitution.*)

verb to take action against something (*Citizens came out to* **protest** *the building of the new skyscraper.*)

Rr

radical (**rad** ih kuhl)
adjective showing extreme beliefs (*Silvia's beliefs are considered* **radical** *in comparison to her parents.*)

noun someone who has extreme beliefs (*The* **radicals** *stood outside of the clothing store to protest the sale of fur.*)

ration (**rash** uhn)
noun a limited amount of something (*The family's* **rations** *were running low, so they talked about how they ought to find more food.*)

verb to limit the amount of something (*After the hurricane, Doug* **rationed** *his canned food to friends and family.*)

react (ree **akt**)
verb to respond in a certain way because of something that has happened to you (*The people of New York City had to* **react** *quickly to the terrorist act.*)

reactionary (ree **ak** shuh **nehr** ee)
adjective wanting to return to an older system (*His plan to take away some of the people's rights was called* **reactionary**.)

noun a person who wants to return to an older system (*The* **reactionaries** *protested against the proposed changes to the law.*)

reform (ri **fawrm**)
verb to improve a law, social system, or institution (*After many years pass, some laws have to be* **reformed** *to keep up with modern standards.*)

noun an improvement in a law, social system, or institution (*The new* **reform** *gave more funding to public schools.*)

refute (ri **fyoot**)
verb to prove that something or someone is wrong (*He tried to* **refute** *the despot and was put in prison for many years.*)

reign (rayn)

verb to rule or have power, especially over a country (*King Tut was believed to have **reigned** over Egypt between 1334 and 1325 B.C.*)

noun the period of time during which someone or a group rules (*During his **reign**, King Henry VIII was married six times.*)

relevant (**rehl** uh vuhnt)

adjective relating to something (*The politician brought up a topic that was not **relevant** to the issue.*)

renaissance (**rehn** uh sawnts)

noun a period of time during which there is a growth in learning and the arts, or the period in Europe from 1400 to 1700 (*Kate enjoys studying **Renaissance** poetry and literature.*)

reparations (rehp uh **ray** shuhns)

noun money paid by losing country to cover damages after a war (*After the war, the **reparations** put the poor country even further in debt.*)

rephrase (ree **frayz**)

verb to say something in a different way (*He was asked to **rephrase** his speech because it was too difficult.*)

republic (ri **puhb** lik)

noun a country where people have the power (*The Congo in Africa is now a democratic **republic**.*)

restate (ree **stayt**)

verb to say or write something again, in a different way (*He was asked to **restate** the last part of his speech in his native language.*)

restoration (**rest** uh **ray** shuhn)

noun the process of bringing something back or making something like new (*The couple did not realize how large a **restoration** project they were in for when they bought the old house.*)

rhetoric (**ret** uhr ik)

noun the use of language to convince people about something (*Plato was famous for his eloquent **rhetoric**.*)

rivalry (**ry** vuhl ree)

noun competition or fighting (*There has been a **rivalry** between the flower shop and the candy store for many years.*)

royalist (**roy** uhl ist)

noun someone who supports rule by a king or queen (*The **royalists** supported King Charles I of England during the war.*)

Ss

sanctions (**sangk** shuhns)

noun actions taken against a country that has broken international laws (*The United States had **sanctions** against Iraq that made it difficult to trade with them.*)

scholar (**skahl** uhr)

noun a person who studies a subject and knows a great deal about it (*After studying literature for thirty years, Tina considered herself a **scholar**.*)

significance (sig **nif** uh kuhns)

noun importance (*The citizens wanted to know the **significance** of the highway reconstruction.*)

socialism (**soh** shuhl **iz** uhm)

noun a system in which the government controls businesses and industries and all people are treated equally (*Domingo believed in **socialism** because he wanted poor people to have opportunities to prosper.*)

sovereign (**sahv** ruhn)

adjective to have the most power, or to be independent, especially in the case of a country (*After the capture of Saddam Hussein, Iraq became a **sovereign** nation.*)

noun a royal ruler of a country (*The **sovereign** lived in a grand castle.*)

strategy (**strat** uh jee)

noun a plan for reaching a goal (*The soldiers came up with a **strategy** to invade the enemy's camp.*)

strike (stryk)

    verb   to stop working until you get better working conditions or pay *(The workers decided to **strike** after inflation took place because they could not longer afford basic necessities.)*

suffrage (**suhf** rij)

    noun   the right to vote for a government or leader *(The Civil Rights movement granted **suffrage** to Americans regardless of race.)*

synthesize (**sin** thuh **syz**)

    verb   to combine information from many sources *(Eli **synthesized** thirty pages of notes from a variety of sources into a six-page report.)*

Tt

tariff (**tar** if)

    noun   a tax that the government collects on imported goods *(The **tariff** on the vase Hugo bought in Spain was more than he expected.)*

territory (**tehr** uh **tawr** ee)

    noun   land controlled by a country or ruler *(The two nations went to war over **territory** that they both claimed.)*

terrorism (**tehr** uhr **iz** uhm)

    noun   acts of violence against civilians *(On September 11, 2001, an act of **terrorism** on the World Trade Center and Pentagon building killed thousands of people.)*

theocracy (thee **ahk** ruh see)

    noun   a society that is ruled by a religious figure *(In a **theocracy**, there is no separation between church and state.)*

totalitarianism (toh **tal** uh **tehr** ee uhn **izm**)

    noun   a system in which one political party controls everything *(**Totalitarianism** is related to fascism and most types of communism.)*

treason (**tree** zuhn)

    noun   an action carried out to harm one's own country *(The man was arrested for **treason** after he was caught revealing top-secret information about his government to another country.)*

Uu

uprising (**uhp ry** zing)

    noun   an act of rebellion, often violent *(An **uprising** of protestors followed the announcement of the war.)*

urbanization (**ur** buhni **zay** shuhn)

    noun   a process in which city populations grow and rural populations shrink *(The world has experienced a great amount of **urbanization** in recent decades.)*

Vv

verify (**vehr** uh **fy**)

    verb   using evidence to check if something is true *(The doctor used a DNA test to **verify** Fernando's identity.)*

visualize (**vizh** oo uhl **yz**)

    verb   to create a picture of something in one's mind *(Since Esteban did not attend the wedding, he had to **visualize** how beautiful the ceremony was.)*

Ww

welfare (**wehl fehr**)

    noun   person's health or comfort, or money paid by the government to unemployed, poor, or sick people *(The government granted **welfare** to the family after the mother lost her job.)*